The Gospel of Peace

Jesus's Teachings of Eternal Truth

Michio Kushi
and Alex Jack

Japan Publications, Inc.

To Peace
Among Nature, Nations,
and Peoples

Published by Japan Publications, Inc., Tokyo and New York

Distributors:
UNITED STATES: Kodansha America, Inc. through Farrar, Straus & Giroux, 19 Union Square West, New York 10003. CANADA: Fitzhenry & Whiteside Ltd., 91 Granton Drive, Richmond Hill, Ontario, L4B 2N5. BRITISH ISLES AND EUROPEAN CONTINENT: Premier Book Marketing Ltd., 1 Gower Street, London WC1E 6HA. AUSTRALIA AND NEW ZEALAND: Bookwise International, 54 Crittenden Road, Findon, South Australia 5023. THE FAR EAST AND JAPAN: JAPAN Publications Trading Co., Ltd., 1–2–1, Sarugaku-cho, Chiyoda-ku, Tokyo 101.

First edition: March 1992

ISBN 0–87040–797–X
LCCC 91–060396

Printed in U.S.A.

Preface

As a child growing up in Japan, I was deeply influenced by the world of spirit and vibration. My ancestors had been Buddhists for some twelve hundred years, and I often visited the family temple in Kumano as well as other temples and shrines where I was living. Once when I was sixteen, as a high school student in Akita City in Honshu in northern Japan, I went to pray and meditate early in the morning before dawn. After some period of meditation—I don't know how long—a golden light filled the room. I walked outside. I noticed that all the trees, grasses, and flowers were shining with a brilliant golden color. I experienced the whole world as a manifestation of God. I experienced everything as alive, radiant, and interconnected. All around me were beautiful swirling spirals of light. Although the immediate experience subsided, from that time on I knew that we were all one and shared a common origin and destiny.

My parents were educators and introduced me to other world religions and cultures. I was particularly attracted to the teachings of Jesus. The Kingdom of Heaven that he described bore a striking resemblance to the world of light and beauty that I had entered. In Akita City, where my parents lived, I taught for a while at the Catholic Holy Ghost Women's High School. When I was drafted into the army, I hid a copy of the Holy Bible in my bags and turned to the Sermon on the Mount and other teachings of Jesus for inspiration and guidance. After the war, I joined the Japanese Protestant Christian Association. In college, I was befriended by Shigeru Nanbara, the Chancellor of Tokyo University; Rev. Toyohiko Kagawa, the educator; and other Christians who were active in the world government movement. My wife, Aveline, came from a pioneer Christian family in Izumo, the mountain province fabled as the home of the Gods.

In the United States, my quest for truth, justice, and peace led me to join the Religious Society of Friends (the Quakers) and the Baptist Church and to study the teachings of the Mormons and other denominations. I also visited Jewish synagogues and Catholic churches and studied the *Upanishads*, the *Qur'an*, and the scriptures of other faiths. I sought out and talked with many great men and women about developing a "Medicine for Humanity" to turn our species from continued war, hatred, and disease.

But no one I talked too, including Norman Cousins, Pitirim Sorokin, Thomas Mann, Upton Sinclair, Robert M. Hutchins, and Albert Einstein, knew how to make human beings more compassionate and altruistic. They encouraged me to find out for myself.

Everyone agreed that unless a way was found to make humanity more peaceful and loving, world government, economic reform, and other structural changes in society would not be enough to save modern civilization. Finally, I quit my graduate studies at Columbia University and set out to observe for myself what made people peaceful or angry, healthy or sick, grateful or spiteful. On the steps of St. Patrick's Cathedral along Fifth Avenue, I spent hours, days, and weeks observing people passing by. What made them alike? What made them different? What governed their destiny? What was the order of life?

At last, I understood. Life is governed by diet and environment. The way we eat largely shapes our day-to-day health and judgment. The way our parents, grandparents, and ancestors ate determines our heredity and constitution. The weather, the seasons, the climate, the geography, the atmosphere, the radiation coming in from the sun, the moon, the stars, and far distant galaxies—all of these influence how we grow and develop, think and behave. Unifying all things—from subatomic particles to galaxies, from colonies of microbes to human civilizations—was a marvelous Order of the Universe. Encouraged by George Ohsawa, a unique Japanese philosopher, I discovered that life moves in a spiral. Opposites attract. Likes repel. From the inside to the outside, from the periphery to the center and then back again, everything was proceeding in harmony according to universal laws and principles.

Since then I have devoted my life to studying and teaching about this wonderful spirallic order, or what we may call the Law of God. Perceiving and acting upon this order or law leads to endless health, prosperity, and spiritual realization and is at the heart of all the world's religions and philosophies, including Buddhism, Judaism, and Christianity. My wife and I are best known for our dietary teachings, but these are just one application of the universal laws of balance and harmony. Macrobiotics—from the traditional Greek words for "Great Life" or "Large Life"—encompasses all aspects of existence including life in this world and the next world; relations between man and woman, parents and children, families and communities, states and nations; the evolution of plants and animals and the development of human consciousness and spirit; the appearance and disappearance of mountains and valleys, cultures and civilizations, comets and cosmos.

Throughout the ages, teachers of life have appeared to guide humanity to higher levels of consciousness and judgment. They have helped people to relieve their suffering and to enter a larger life of health, happiness, and peace. However, their teachings have often been lost, altered, or misunderstood. Over the centuries, great religions have been founded in their names. These, in turn, have splintered into rival denominations and sects. Each group has its own scriptures and rituals, techniques and traditions. So much has been added, subtracted, or changed that it is very difficult today to hear the true voice of Jesus or Buddha.

In the case of Jesus, our understanding has been enriched by two recent findings. In 1945, the Nag Hammadi Library was discovered in Egypt, and in 1947 the Dead Sea Scrolls were found in Palestine. Among the scores of ancient manuscripts that came to light was a spiritual masterpiece—the *Gospel of Thomas*. Because of its seemingly mysterious sayings and parables, people were slow to recognize its significance. In 1959 when it was first translated into English, I realized that the *Gospel of Thomas* was based on the unifying principle of macrobiotics—an understanding of the infinite Order of the Universe, or what Jesus called the Justice of the Kingdom of God. I marveled that the *Gospel of Thomas* was not only the deepest, most authentic expression of Jesus's teachings, but also it unlocked the meaning of many of the central concepts and teachings in the New Testament that had long puzzled me. Here was the true key to Jesus's life and thought.

I immediately translated the *Gospel of Thomas* into Japanese and sent it to George Ohsawa with whom I had studied macrobiotics in Japan. Unfortunately, the manuscript was lost, and it was a long time before the *Gospel of Thomas* was published in Japan.

In Boston, I started to use the *Gospel of Thomas* in my classes. Over the last twenty-five years, I have referred to it countless times, taking an afternoon or evening to read and discuss it with my students, saying by saying. In my Spiritual Development Seminars at the Kushi Institute in the Berkshire Mountains, the *Gospel of Thomas* has become a principal text, along with the Bible, the *Tao Te Ching*, the *Heart Sutra*, and the scriptures of other world religions.

Jesus spoke in parables and made use of symbol, allegory, and paradox. He did this to let his disciples discover truth for themselves. Like Socrates and other teachers of life, he answered his students' questions with questions of his own. This is the best way to let people grow and develop. If you answer their questions directly, you deprive them of the adventure and satisfaction of discovering the answers for themselves. And instead of becoming strong, independent, and free, they grow dependent on you.

I try to follow this traditional way of teaching in my classes. In studying the *Gospel of Thomas*, we generally take one saying and read it out loud together once or twice. Then I ask people what they think it means. We go around the room with everyone free to express his or her opinion. If someone is on the right track, I will question them until they understand. If someone is off the mark, I will try to bring them back. In this way, the class as a whole is guided toward the meaning of the passage. Gradually their consciousness grows and their understanding deepens. A spirit of wonder, awe, and self-discovery is cultivated.

Meanwhile, these macrobiotic friends are eating very simply, usually just whole grain as principal food, with some beans and vegetables, and some fish occasionally and very little fruit. This is the kind of food that Jesus and his disciples ate together, so naturally they begin to develop a similar mentality. If you really want to understand someone, you need only to eat the same food they eat. Buddha, Lao Tzu, Moses, Jesus, Mohammed, and other teachers of humanity all ate very simply, mostly grains and vegetables. If we follow their way of eating, it's not hard to discover their true teachings. We can have the same image and the same thoughts. This is the best way to understand Jesus, to become like a brother to him, a friend.

For those who have not read the *Gospel of Thomas* before, I strongly encourage you to read the text on your own several times before looking at the commentary. Seek to figure out for yourself what Jesus was trying to say. It's really very easy to understand. But your own intuition has to be sharp. Your condition has to be clear and clean. You have to be eating well. Then you don't need this commentary. You will see into Jesus's heart directly.

Alex Jack, co-author of *The Cancer-Prevention Diet, Diet for a Strong Heart*, and *One Peaceful World*, has prepared this book with me. Alex has a background in religion and philosophy and has written a series of articles on Jesus for the *East West Journal* where he served as editor. I appreciate very much his help and devotion to making these teachings of peace and harmony more widely available.

This book deals primarily with Jesus's cosmology and view of life in the *Gospel of Thomas*. In the future, we plan to write another volume, focusing on Jesus's dietary and healing prac-

10

tices in the New Testament. The third and final work in this series would then discuss Jesus's prophetic teachings and view of
human destiny in the Gospels and *Book of Revelation*.

Alex and I are grateful to our wives and families for their love
and care over the last seven years during the preparation of this
manuscript, to our associates at the Kushi Institute and One
Peaceful World, and to Mr. Iwao Yoshizaki and Mr. Yoshiro
Fujiwara, president and vice-president of Japan Publications,
Inc., our publishers, for their unfailing support and encourage-
ment.

I pray that everyone will take time to reflect on the spiritual
teachings presented in these pages and put them into practice in
their daily lives. Together let us live in the Kingdom of Heaven,
let us realize one healthy, peaceful world.

Michio Kushi
Becket, Massachusetts
July, 1991

Contents

List of Tables and Illustrations

14

Introduction: *The Spiral of Life*

Until the discovery of the *Gospel of Thomas*, our knowledge of Jesus's teachings came primarily from the Holy Bible. The writings of Matthew, Mark, Luke, and John are believed to have been based on oral accounts or on earlier written collections of Jesus's sayings. According to historians, the four Gospels were composed during the second half of the first century, or some one to two generations after the events they describe. The New Testament itself was not compiled until several hundred years later from a much larger group of texts in circulation at that period.

Foremost among the writings left out of the New Testament was the *Gospel of Thomas*. Like many other early works, it was suppressed, and efforts were made by Church officials to destroy all remaining copies. They succeeded, and for nearly sixteen hundred years, the *Gospel of Thomas* was lost. Its existence was known only from mention in the writings of the early Church Fathers and from scattered quotations that survived in the original Greek.

Recovery of the Gospel of Thomas: In 1945, an ancient library of manuscripts was discovered in Egypt, including a Coptic translation of the *Gospel of Thomas*. One day, two brothers set out in quest of nitrates to use as fertilizer in their fields. By the cliffs near a bend in the Nile River between Nag Hammadi and Luxor, they came upon a large ceramic jar hidden beneath a boulder. At first they were hesitant to open the jar because they feared it might contain an evil spirit. But thinking that it contained gold, the elder brother smashed the jar with his mattock. Golden particles spiraled out and vanished in the sky. The particles were specks of parchment. Inside the jar they discovered thirteen old books wrapped in leather. The young men returned on their camels to their village with the fragile manuscripts wrapped in a tunic. Because the parchments were so faded and brittle, they did not recognize the value of their treasure. The old books were left in the courtyard among the straw to be burned in the large clay oven where bread was baked. Their mother used some of the parchment and the covers for this purpose. But the bulk of the texts survived.

Over the next several years, rumors of the find reached scholars and antiquity dealers in Cairo, 370 miles to the north. A period of intrigue followed, involving museum curators, academics, and smugglers on several continents. One codex found its way into the hands of psychologist Carl Jung in Zurich, who had written about early Christianity and recognized its significance.

Eventually, all of the texts were returned to Egypt where, in 1956, an international commission of scholars began the work of preserving, cataloguing, and translating them. Together they became known as the Nag Hammadi Library, after the Egyptian town near where they were found. The thirteen volumes contained fifty-two individual texts covering more than 1,100 pages. They are written in Coptic, an Egyptian language that uses primarily Greek letters. Arabic replaced Coptic as the common tongue in Egypt about a thousand years ago, but Coptic is still used in the liturgy of the Coptic Church.

The texts are all believed to be translations from originals in Greek. According to scholars, they date from the third and fourth centuries A.D. However, the originals are believed to be older. Many types of literature are represented in the Nag Hammadi Library, including gospels, acts, apocalypses, dialogues, letters, treatises, exegeses, prayers, and hymns.

Many of the texts are associated with Gnosticism, a religious movement that flourished in the second and third centuries. *Gnosis* is the Greek word for "knowledge." Gnostics believed that they had true knowledge of reality and lived in a world of light unlike members of other religions whom they characterized as living in darkness. Our modern word *agnostic* comes from this source and means someone without knowledge. There were various types of Gnostics. Some Gnostics considered themselves Christian, some Jewish, and others were affiliated with the Roman, Egyptian, or Middle Eastern mystery cults that grew up at the time. But almost all Gnostics believed in a divine spark that fell into the world of matter. The Nag Hammadi texts contain many Gnostic myths and accounts, including the creation of the world by a Demiurge, the fall of Sophia (Wisdom), and the cosmic ascent and descent of Christ through a hierarchy of hostile forces. There are also several non-Gnostic works in the Nag Hammadi collection, including a Christian wisdom text, *The Teachings of Silvanus*, and a section from Plato's *The Republic*.

The manuscripts are believed to have been copied in one of the monasteries of St. Pachomius, which were then located near Nag Hammadi. In about A.D. 367, the Coptic Patriarch in Alexandria instigated a purge against all unauthorized teachings, and the abbot of the monastery may have ordered that all books not included in the Bible be destroyed. There was a garrison of Roman soldiers across the river from the monastery which would have been instructed to enforce the edict. The texts may have been placed in the ceramic jar at this time for safekeeping and hidden in the white cliffs near the Nile.

Although Gnostic cosmology is absent from its text, the *Gospel of Thomas* was initially classified as a Gnostic scripture on account of its discovery amid a library of mostly Gnostic works and because of its seemingly enigmatic vocabulary. In the *Gospel of Thomas*, Jesus speaks about light and darkness, body and soul, spirit and matter, and other polarities that appear to share a Gnostic theme and interpretation. There are also mysterious references to "the Living One," "Five trees in Paradise," "the sign of the Father," and other terms that have no obvious counterpart in the Bible.

On the other hand, the *Gospel of Thomas* contained fifteen of Jesus's parables, including thirteen that are found in the New Testament. It also included material on the Kingdom of Heaven; the Father, Son, and Holy Spirit; the Chosen; the Logos; the Cross; and other basic concepts. Many of Thomas's passages that did not have parallels or echoes in the Bible appeared to have an authentic cadence and rhythm. Clearly, the *Gospel of Thomas* was the most important of all the texts found at Nag Hammadi, and it began to attract international attention.

Over the last thirty years, historians and Bible experts have largely reversed their original assessment. The emerging consensus is that the *Gospel of Thomas* is not Gnostic at all but is the earliest of all the Christian gospels and preserves Jesus's teachings in the simplest, most original form. "If one considers the form and wording of the individual sayings in comparison with the form in which they are preserved in the New Testament," observes Professor Helmut Koester of Harvard Divinity School, "*The Gospel of Thomas* almost always appears to have preserved a more original form of the traditional saying . . ." Its vocabulary turned out to be no more esoteric than the *Gospel of John* which also deals with light and darkness and other themes later developed by the Gnostics. The date of the *Gospel of Thomas* also has steadily been pushed back. Some historians now believe that it was composed as early as A.D. 50. That would be within the lifetime of the Apostle Thomas and decades earlier than the New Testament Gospels.

The Apostle Thomas: In the prologue, the editor of the *Gospel of Thomas* introduces himself as Didymus Judas Thomas. *Didymus* is Greek for "twin," and *Thomas* is Aramaic for "twin." Literally his name means "Twin Judas Twin." A legend grew up in the Middle East that Thomas was the twin brother of Jesus. Some commentators have accepted Thomas as Jesus's biological twin. Others regard it as signifying that Thomas was the highest of all the disciples and became Jesus's spiritual twin, or equal to him in understanding.

Thomas appears in all four gospels in the New Testament. He is best known as Doubting Thomas, the apostle who remained skeptical of Jesus's resurrection until he felt the scars of the crucifixion for himself. Thomas also played a role in the story of the healing of Lazarus. He appeared at the Last Supper and asked the question that inspired Jesus to proclaim, "I am the way, and the truth, and the life." After Easter Sunday, Thomas joined the other disciples in picking a successor to Judas, and later he was among the seven disciples who went fishing and came upon Jesus on the shore of the Sea of Galilee.

According to tradition, after Jesus's death, the twelve apostles cast lots to determine the region of the world each would go to spread the teachings. Thomas is credited with bringing Christianity to Mesopotamia, and historians think that the *Gospel of Thomas* was probably composed in Edessa, a major city on the ancient caravan route between East and West. Thomas is then said to have gone to India where he taught for many years and died. A fanciful account of his travels is preserved in *The Acts of Thomas*, composed in Greek and Syrian about A.D. 200. In the thirteenth century, Marco Polo visited Madras, in Southern India, and reported visiting a church dedicated to St. Thomas. During the war in the Persian Gulf in 1991, the Church of St. Thomas in Mosul—the oldest Christian church in Iraq (ancient Mesopotamia) dating to the fourth century—was bombed and damaged.

Content of the Gospel of Thomas: The *Gospel of Thomas* consists of 114 sayings of Jesus, usually beginning with "Jesus said," or "The disciples asked him." The numbering is not found in the original manuscript. For convenience' sake, scholars have numbered the text in the way that the Bible has been divided into chapters and verses. The sayings in the *Gospel of Thomas* are universal and apply to all people, times, and places. They are as true today as when they were uttered. The *Gospel of John* also includes wisdom sayings, possibly derived from a source also known to Thomas.

Collections of wisdom sayings were very popular in the ancient world. Old Testament examples include the *Book of Proverbs*, the *Wisdom of Solomon, Ecclesiastes*, and parts of the *Book of Job*. In the New Testament, the Sermon on the Mount is such a collection of teachings. The *Gospels of Matthew* and

Luke are believed to incorporate another lost collection of Jesus's sayings known as *Q* (from the German word *Quelle* meaning source document). The *Gospel of John* includes wisdom sayings, possibly derived from a source also known to Thomas.

In the *Gospel of Thomas*, Jesus appears purely as a wise teacher of life. His disciples continually speculate whether he is the expected Messiah or Christ. But except for the term Son of Man which also is found in the New Testament, he does not identify himself with any messianic figure.

Unlike the other gospels, there are virtually no narrative details about Jesus's life or death in the *Gospel of Thomas*. There is no mention of the crucifixion or resurrection. Besides Thomas, several other disciples or students appear in the text, including James the Just, Simon Peter, Matthew, Salome, and Mary (presumably Mary Magdalene). Also Jesus talks about John the Baptist, Adam, the Prophets, the Scribes and Pharisees, a Samaritan, Caesar, his mother, father, and brothers, and other familiar figures from the Bible.

As in the four gospels, Jesus's teachings in the *Gospel of Thomas* are drawn from everyday life and include stories about farmers, fishermen, physicians, blind men, the wealthy, the poor, merchants, robbers, assassins, harlots, and little children. The natural world also assumes a prominent role. There are parables and proverbs dealing with seeds, crops, soil, wood, mountains, stones, pearls, and thorns. Among food and drink, Jesus mentions wheat and other grains, bread and flour, grapes and figs, wine and water. Among animals, he talks about birds, fish, lions, serpents, doves, horses, worms, lambs, moths, pigs, dogs, oxen, sheep, and foxes. There are images of city and desert, banquets and fasting, marriage celebration and solitary prayer.

Jesus's Background and View of Life: Jesus came from a very modest family. The reason he developed into such a supremely enlightened person was that his mother, Mary, was a very humble woman. His father, Joseph, was also humble and hard-working. When her baby was in the womb, Mary was very active and she had to travel. Jesus was born, not at home, but on a journey. Mary was very hard-working and active—what in Far Eastern philosophy we call very yang. She ate very simple food. So naturally her baby was born with a strong constitution and was healthy. Also while he was growing up, Jesus's family had to struggle for what they needed. In comparison with most of us today, his family was very poor. First, during the flight to Egypt, and then while living in Nazareth, they had little money and had to work hard for their food and their home. Our life today in modern civilized society is so soft and so rich—so yin—in comparison with the life they had to live. But this poverty helped to create strong persons. Jesus was a very strong man.

At the same time Israel was in the control of a foreign power. This subjugation of the country is another factor leading to the development of a spiritual leader among the people. Further, the Middle East has a very warm climate. People living in a tropical or semi-tropical environment tend to be more mentally and spiritually active—or more yin in their orientation (*see* Table 1). To balance the hot weather, they are attracted to fruit, oil, sweets, and hot, spicy foods. There is a tendency toward leprosy, epilepsy, possession, and other more yin type of diseases. Philosophically, there is a tendency toward esoteric, mystical, complex thinking. Compared to the people around him, Jesus was much more yang. He ate a very simple diet, prayed and fasted, walked long distances, and was very physically active. His expression was very simple, short, and down-to-earth.

There are many gaps in Jesus's life. There is an unkown period of eighteen years between the time he studied with the elders at the Temple in Jerusalem as a child and when he started to teach and heal people of their illnesses. During this time, he may have worked as a carpenter, helped in the fields and pastures, and traveled. In the wilderness, where he fasted for forty days, Jesus further strengthened—yangized—himself and had occasion to contemplate the night sky and master the order of nature.

Central to Jesus's world view was an understanding of the logarithmic spiral. This basic form, which appears throughout

22

Table 1. Examples of Yin and Yang.

	Yin ∇*	Yang Δ*
Attribute	Centrifugal force	Centripetal force
Tendency	Expansion	Contraction
Function	Diffusion	Fusion
	Dispersion	Assimilation
	Separation	Gathering
	Decomposition	Organization
Movement	More inactive, slower	More active, faster
Vibration	Shorter wave and higher frequency	Longer wave and lower frequency
Direction	More outward and peripheral	More inward and central
Weight	Lighter	Heavier
Temperature	Colder	Hotter
Light	Darker	Brighter
Humidity	Wetter	Drier
Density	Thinner	Thicker
Size	Larger	Smaller
Shape	More expansive and fragile	More contractive and harder
Texture	Softer	Harder
Atomic particle	N, O, P, Ca, etc.	H, C, Na, As, Mg, etc.
Environrnent	Vibration . . . Air . . . Water . . . Earth	
Climatic effects	Tropical climate	Colder climate
Biological	More vegetable quality	More anirnal quality
Sex	Female	Male
Organ structure	More hollow and expansive	More compacted and condensed
Nerves	More peripheral, orthosympathetic	More central, parasympathetic
Attitude emotion	More gentle, negative, defensive	More active, positive, aggressive
Work	More psychological and mental	More physical and social
Consciousness	More universal	More specific
Mental function	Dealing more with the future	Dealing more with the past
Culture	More spiritually oriented	More materially oriented
Dimension	Space	Time

* For convenience, the symbols ∇ for Yin, and Δ for Yang are used.

nature, reveals the mechanism of creation and the fundamental unity and interconnectedness of life. This simple but comprehensive form can be observed in all things, including seashells and spider webs, the currents of wind and water, the growth and development of trees, flowers, and plants, and the formation of galaxies. The spiral construction of the universe has left many traces within the human form, including the basic shape of the embryo, the formation of our ears, the development of arms and legs, the coiling of our intestines, the whorls of our fingertips, and the spiral pattern of hair growing on the back of our heads. Modern science has discovered this form in the double-helix, the spiral-shaped chromosomes in each and every cell.

From the surface of the earth to the reaches of outer space, logarithmic spirals appear and disappear in all dimensions of the boundless ocean of universal energy. Our world of change governed by two antagonistic and complementary forces, yin and yang, is the relative world sensed, perceived, and experienced by everyone in daily life. From a tiny seed in the field to large movements of the entire universe, every phenomenon is spirally governed between expansion and contraction, in the relation of front and back, of inner and outer, and in the balance between the beginning and the end.

Throughout the ancient world, people traditionally believed that life unfolded in a dynamic cycle or spiral. From God or the infinite universe, all life in the cosmos came into being, and after a long winding journey through many planes of existence all life returned to its eternal source. The levels of being—or heavens —were usually numbered as seven.

In the *Book of Genesis*, this is symbolized by the seven days or stages of creation (*see* Figure 1). In the beginning, the earth was void and without form.This is the first stage, the unmanifest. Then God created the heaven and the earth—time and space, centripetality and centrifugality, the force of contraction and expansion, yang and yin. Polarity is the second stage. Then God created light and darkness, or the world of vibration. This is the third stage. Then God created the firmament above the earth.

24

Figure 1. The Seven Days of Creation in Genesis.

1. The Void
2. Heaven and Earth
3. Light and Darkness
4. The Firmament
5. Dry Land and Water
6. Grass and Herb-Bearing Seeds
7. Birds, Animals, Creeping Things, Adam and Eve

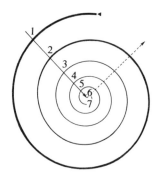

Today this is what we would call the world of subatomic particles and the ionosphere. This is the fourth stage. Then God created dry land and water, or the world of elements. This is the fifth stage. Then God created the grass and herb-bearing seeds. This is the world of plants, the sixth stage. Finally God created creatures in the water, on the earth, and in the air, including Adam and Eve, representing the first man and woman. This is the animal kingdom culminating in humanity, the seventh and last stage of creation.

After becoming human beings, the most condensed or centripetal species of life, we start our return journey to union with God or the infinite universe. In this part of the journey, we develop and refine our consciousness. We grow in a centrifugal direction, passing through seven stages of expanding awareness (*see* Figure 2). From mechanical judgment or spontaneous, unconscious action, we graduate to sensory judgment. In this level, we develop and master the five senses. Then at the third level, that of emotional judgment, we develop aesthetic likes and dislikes and form romantic attachments. At the fourth level, we refine our mind and intellect. At the fifth level, we become aware of the world of nature and society around us. At the sixth level, we enter the realm of philosophy and seek answers to spiritual questions. Finally, at the seventh level, we become one

Figure 2. The Seven Stages of Consciousness.

1. Mechanical Consciousness
2. Sensory Consciousness
3. Emotional Consciousness
4. Intellectual Consciousness
5. Social Consciousness
6. Philosophical Consciousness
7. Universal Consciousness

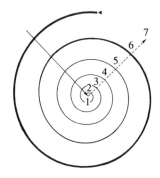

with God and the infinite universe itself. In the Bible, this return half of the journey was symbolized by Jacob's dream of ascending a great ladder or spiral staircase reaching up to heaven.

Other symbols of the spiral in the Bible include the burning bush in which God appeared to Moses, the pillar of fire and cloud that led the children of Israel through the wilderness, the circle of fire that fell from the sky on Mount Carmel at the behest of Elijah, the wheels that Ezekiel saw next to the throne of God, the voice that came out of a whirlwind to speak to Job, the dove that descended over Jesus when he was baptized in the River Jordan, the curling tongues of flame that alighted on the heads of those at Pentecost, and St. John the Divine's vision of the rolling up of the cosmos like a scroll at the end of time. Whenever the people forgot their spiritual origin or destiny, a spiral image would appear to guide and inspire them. In the ancient world, spirals were inscribed on walls and rocks and appeared in paintings and cooking vessels. From Ice Age caves to Egyptian murals, from Mesoamerican pyramids to Celtic manuscripts, from Greek pottery to Chinese brocade, spirals have been carved, drawn, or woven by generation after generation to express their understanding and appreciation of the universal pattern of change that connects all things. Jesus refers to this spirallic process as the Kingdom of Heaven. From seed to harvest, from leaven to loaf, from knowledge to wisdom, everything unfolds in an orderly way. One level leads organically to the next, step by step, stage by stage, heaven by heaven.

In macrobiotics today, we talk about the Order of the Universe, the supreme, eternal, invincible order that governs all things. It is exactly the same thing as the Kingdom of Heaven.

This is the cosmological background to Jesus's teachings. Again and again in the *Gospel of Thomas* he makes reference to the moving, changing endless circle of life. This is what he is trying to make people see, the big view, the larger life—*makrobios*. We can almost see him kneeling down to draw a spiral on the ground or in the sand to illustrate a point when he instructs his students or takes issue with the Scribes and Pharisees. In passage after passage, he teaches his disciples to identify with the Father, or infinite source of life. By acting from that place, they can become healthy and happy, free and whole. By unifying opposites—motion and rest, above and below, inner and outer—they can endlessly realize their endless dream.

To help modern readers understand Jesus's view of life in the *Gospel of Thomas*, we have included spiral diagrams and labels whenever appropriate. The spiral can be represented in many ways, including the Star of David and the Cross. The spiral—or unifying principle, as it is also called—is the key to Jesus's spiritual teachings. Once we understand his view of life in the *Gospel of Thomas*, it is easier to interpret the New Testament, which was compiled by a later generation that did not understand the Kingdom of Heaven and had forgotten its spirallic order.

"Macrobiotics" in the Bible: The ordinary everyday language in Jesus's time was Aramaic. Hebrew had become a dead language following the Babylonian Captivity six hundred years earlier. When Ezra read the scriptures to the people in Jerusalem after the exile, he had to translate them into Aramaic. A form of Hebrew was revived but was spoken only among priests and scholars. Aramaic, the official language of the Persian Empire,

was spoken in daily conversation in Judea, Galilee, and other regions. Many people also had a working knowledge of Greek, the *lingua franca* of politics, commerce, and literature throughout the Hellenistic world.

After the exile, the Temple was rebuilt in Jerusalem, but the nation remained divided. Into the first century of the present era, a majority of the Jewish people continued to live outside of Israel in Italy, Egypt, Greece, Asia Minor, and other areas of the Roman Empire. Since they had forgotten how to read and speak Hebrew, the Bible was translated into Greek, the language of the educated. This Bible became known as the *Septuagint*. Prepared by seventy Hebrew scholars, it was completed in the third century B.C. The *Septuagint* was the most widely used Bible in the Mediterranean world in Jesus's day, and it became the Old Testament of the early Christian Church.

Jesus appears to have spoken Aramaic, Hebrew, and Greek. He is depicted as reading the scriptures (probably in the original Hebrew), debating the scribes (who spoke a revived form of Hebrew), teaching the multitudes (who spoke in Aramaic), and conversing with the Romans (who spoke Greek and wrote in Latin). It is also likely that most of his disciples spoke Aramaic and had some knowledge of Greek. The *Gospel of Thomas* and New Testament were originally composed in Greek.

The question arises whether Jesus was familiar with the term *makrobios*—or macrobiotics—in Greek. The word is derived from the common Greek words *makro*, meaning "long" or "large," and bios, meaning "life" or "living." *Makrobios* literally meant "long life" or "longevity" and in the classical world came to be broadly identified with a simple, natural way of life and eating. It had been first used in the fourth century B.C. by Hippocrates, the Father of Medicine, whose philosophy of life was "Let food be thy medicine, and medicine thy food." Herodotus, Lucian, Aristotle, Galen, and other classical writers also used the term *makrobios* as did Clement and other early Church Fathers.

Although it does not appear in the New Testament, the word *makrobios* appears several times in the Greek translation of the

Hebrew Bible, the *Septuagint*. In the *Book of Baruch*, composed by Jeremiah's secretary, we read:

> Why is it, Israel, that you are in your enemies' country, that you have grown old in an alien land? Why have you shared the defilement of the dead and been numbered with those that lie in the grave? It is because you have forsaken the fountain of wisdom. If you had walked in the way of God, you would have lived in peace for ever. Where is understanding, where is strength, where is intelligence? Learn that, and then you will know where to find life and light to walk by, long life [*makrobios*] and peace.—Baruch 3:9-14

The word *makrobios* also appears in the *Wisdom of Solomon*, and there is a variant of the term in *Proverbs*. In Greek, a well-known passage on wisdom reads:

> Length of days [macrobiotics] is in her right hand; and in her left hand riches and honor.
> Her ways are ways of pleasantness, and all her paths are peace.
>
> —Proverbs 3.17

But possibly the most significant reference to macrobiotics is in the *Book of Isaiah:*

> And he, because of his affliction, opens not his mouth: he was led as a sheep to the slaughter, and as a lamb before the shearer is dumb, so he opens not his mouth. In *his* humiliation his judgment was taken away: who shall declare his generation? for his life is taken away from the earth: because of the iniquities of my people he was led to death. And I will give the wicked for his burial, and the rich for his death; for he practised no iniquity, nor craft with his mouth. The Lord also is pleased to purge him from his stroke. If ye can give an offering for sin, your soul shall see

a long-lived [*makrobios*] seed: the Lord also is pleased to take away from the travail of his soul, to shew him light; and to form *him* with understanding; to justify the just one who serves many well; and he shall bear their sins.—*Isaiah 53:7–11*

This passage, one of the most famous in the Bible, deals with what has come to be known as the Suffering Servant. Jews have traditionally viewed the Suffering Servant as Israel. They believe Isaiah's prophecy refers to a future Israel which righteously upholds the teachings of the Law (the Torah) in the face of foreign domination and conquest. After a period of great trial and tribulation, Israel will emerge triumphant and serve as an example for the healing of the nations. Christians have identified Jesus with the Suffering Servant. They view Isaiah's words as foretelling his life, death, and resurrection. The idea in both cases is that patience, love, and grateful acceptance of difficulties and suffering, as opposed to physical might and violent resistance, will lead to salvation.

Whether or not he used the word *makrobios*, Jesus embodies the spirit of living life from the largest view—that of the endless Order of the Universe, the Kingdom of Heaven.

The Gospel of Thomas

Text and Commentary

A Note on the Translation: In the past thirty years, there have
been numerous translations of the *Gospel of Thomas* into English. Some are very literal and straightforward, others more lofty
and poetic. Some are more archaic in their expression, with
"thees" and "thous," others are more colloquial. Some convey a
very down-to-earth Jesus, others an other-worldly Christ. We
have tried to strike a balance, presenting Jesus's teachings in a
simple, clear, direct way. At the same time, we have tried to
preserve some of the traditional rhythms and cadences of the
New Testament gospels, especially in parables, beatitudes, and
other parallel sayings.

It should be noted that Coptic does not differentiate between
upper and lower case letters, and there is no punctuation or numbering in the original. We have capitalized Kingdom of Heaven,
Son of Man, Holy Spirit, and other key concepts. We have also
capitalized Me and Mine in some cases, as explained in the commentary below, where Jesus acts as a representative of universal
Oneness. Brackets [ ] indicate a gap or text that is missing or
unclear and which has been supplied according to our best judgment.

During the last nearly two thousand years, Jesus's words have
passed through many tongues—Hebrew, Aramaic, Greek, Latin,
Coptic, English and other modern languages—and through
many hands—disciples, theologians, editors, and translators. It
is a marvel of marvels that despite all of these intermediaries,
Jesus's spirit continues to shine, speaking to our innermost
hearts.

Quotations from the Bible are from the King James Version
unless otherwise stated.

**Prologue. These are the hidden words that the living Jesus
spoke and Didymos Judas Thomas wrote down.**

In reality, there are no secrets in the universe. Nothing is hidden.
Truth is always present. But because our minds are clouded, we

do not understand the true nature of life. We see, but we do not know. We feel, touch, and read but do not understand. For example, before learning visual diagnosis, you saw the facial features of many people, but you did not understand what different colorations, marks, shapes, and sizes signified. You didn't notice many things about their health and destiny, although they were right in front of you all the time. Before you learned macrobiotic diagnosis, that was a secret for you. It depends on your understanding. For those who understand, there are no secrets. For those who do not understand, sometimes a teacher is necessary to guide and inspire them. Jesus is such a teacher of life. Spirit is eternal. His words are always true—or living—and can instruct us in the permanent, invincible order of the infinite universe.

1. And he said, "Whoever finds the meaning of these words shall not taste death."

If you truly understand Jesus's teachings, you will know that life is eternal. There is no death, just transformation.

The metaphor "will not taste death" is used five times in the *Gospel of Thomas*. It is also found in the *Gospel of John*: "If a man keeps my saying, he shall never taste death." [*John* 8:52] There is no end, just change. Whoever understands this will not experience death. He or she will know the eternally changing world.

2. Jesus said, "Let him who seeks not stop seeking until he finds, and when he finds, he will be troubled, and when he has been troubled, he will be astonished, and he will reign over the Whole."

When we find the Order of the Universe, we will be troubled. First we will be troubled over our own past. We will see that it was not worthwhile, and now we have to change our view and way of life, including the way of eating. Second, when we start to find out the truth, we will be troubled. So many things seem to be confusing. So many people disagree with what we are beginning to learn. We begin to doubt our new-found understanding in the face of all this opposition. Third, other people may cause trouble for us. Our life may appear so strange or different that we are criticized or accused. We may eat a different way. We may not follow the conventional way a majority is practicing. We may not want to fight in a war. The mainstream of society may turn against us, as early Christians experienced. Fourth, we will be troubled on account of our family and friends who are going in a seemingly opposite direction. We see clearly the sickness and suffering they are bringing upon themselves but are not able to change their way of life.

But once we have experienced this being "troubled" and begin to see the light behind it, then we will really begin to marvel. We will be so surprised to see how we are getting better and better. Our health will be improved, our understanding will deepen, and we will finally be able to reign over everything. We find that by changing our own condition, we can influence those around us. They will change as a result of our unfailing health, spirit of humbleness and modesty, and merry, good humor. We are no longer troubled, confused, angry, or feeling misunderstood. We really understand the Order of the Universe and marvel that everything—including sickness, unhappiness, and war— is part of the invincible order of nature. We are amazed and embrace life in all its manifestations. We eventually establish our self in harmony with God or One Infinity and become king, ruling spiritually over all.

3. Jesus said: "If those who guide you say to you: 'See, the kingdom is in heaven,' then the birds of the air will precede you. If they say to you: 'It is in the sea,' then the fishes of the deep will precede you. Rather, the Kingdom is within you and without you. If you would know yourselves, you will be known. You will know that you are the children of the Living Father. But if you do not know yourselves, you dwell in poverty and you are the poverty."

The Kingdom of Heaven: what is it? A kingdom is a country that has order. It is God's country or the Order of the Infinite Universe. This invincible order is not bounded by heaven or by the sea. It is not just in the heart or soul. Order is everywhere. It is all around us, inside and out. It is not just in the distant past or far future. It is now and always. The Kingdom of Heaven encompasses this earth, the sky and solar system, the universe as a whole, everything. This is a big contrast from the teaching of the churches. They think someday the Kingdom of Heaven will come. The Living Father: who is it? *Living* means eternally active, alive, changing, moving. *Father* means source or origin of life. The Living Father is the infinite universe, the source and end of all life. To "know yourselves" is to know where you came from, where you are, and where you are going.

Jesus teaches that we are all children of the Living Father or the infinite universe. He is not the only son of God. That was misunderstood by the later Church. Christianity has taught that Jesus will come back and establish order. Order is already there, only we don't perceive it.

Those who know their infinite origin are infinitely rich. Their world is limitless. But those who do not know are very poor. Their world is very small. They forgot the wonderful Kingdom of Heaven. Even if you rule the entire Roman Empire, that can't compare with knowledge of your infinite origin and destiny. Such a person is living in poverty.

4. Jesus said: "The man old in days will not hesitate to ask a little child of seven days about the place of Life, and he shall live. For many who are first shall be last and they shall be a solitary one."

All are governed by the same spirallic laws of change and harmony. Everyone is going in the same way. In this saying, the image is of an old person not hesitating to watch a young baby to learn the secret of life. The old man is wondering what will happen when he dies. He fears maybe this is the end or that he will go to hell or paradise. By observing a newborn baby, he can understand where he is going. The place must be the same. The baby came from that world where he will soon go.

In this passage, Jesus is referring here to the Spiral of Life (*see* Figure 3). This is the cosmological background to his teachings. In our journey from One Infinity to life on this earth and back to One Infinity, we pass through many levels of existence, constantly refining our consciousness and judgment. In the ancient Holy Land and Far East, this gave rise to the doctrine of reincarnation. The person who understands the Spiral of Life knows that life is eternal.

Figure 3. The Spiral of Life.

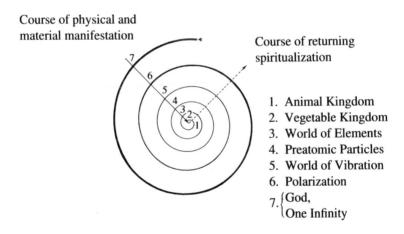

Course of physical and material manifestation

Course of returning spiritualization

1. Animal Kingdom
2. Vegetable Kingdom
3. World of Elements
4. Preatomic Particles
5. World of Vibration
6. Polarization
7. God, One Infinity

If our body and consciousness are clean and clear, we can know a lot about our own infinite nature. However, if we are not clean and clear through our daily life, including eating well, we will get confused and deteriorate in both mind and body and can no longer watch, think, and discover. According to the structure of time, which moves and changes spirally, our offspring become our ancestors. Our ancestors become our offspring. That is the structure of the Kingdom of Heaven, of life. The Kingdom of Heaven is not plain or flat. It is not a circle. It is a spiral.

From the periphery you go to the center; from the center you go
to the periphery. You constantly appear and disappear. That is
the cycle of life.

The first shall be last, and the last shall be first. Those who
are ahead will fall behind, and those who follow shall lead. Life
is one. Everyone is both a teacher and student. To become a
solitary one means to find eternal life, to become one with God
or One Infinity. For that, we must constantly learn from each
other. Young or old, male or female, rich or poor, high or low,
we are all sons and daughters—ones manifested out—of and
within the infinite universe, sharing a common origin and destiny.

**5. Jesus said: "Know what is in your sight, and what is hid-
den from you will come to light. For there is nothing hidden
that shall not be revealed."**

A marvelous order governs daily life, including patterns of
health and sickness, happiness and unhappiness, growth and
decay. By observing our surroundings, we can come to know
everything. Before, we didn't notice this wonderful order. Now
as our own health and judgment improve, it becomes abundantly
clear. We begin to see the front and back or visible and invisible
sides of all phenomena. We start to see their beginning and end.
Everything around us reveals the Order of the Infinite Universe.
One practical application of this marvelous order is visual diagnosis or physiognomy, the traditional art of seeing character and
destiny by observing the face and features of the body. Through
visual diagnosis, we can see internal problems long before they
develop into outward symptoms. Then we can make appropriate
dietary or way of life changes to bring ourselves back in harmony with nature. This method was known in the ancient
Middle East, Greece, and the Far East and was used by Jesus
and his students to diagnose and heal people. But to most
people, then as now, that order remains hidden and goes un-
noticed. They do not see infinity, or the marvelous Kingdom of

Heaven around them, and can only look at simple, natural ways of diagnosing and healing as miracles.

6. His disciples asked and said to him: "Do you wish us to fast?" "And how shall we pray?" "And shall we bestow alms?" "And what diet shall we follow?" Jesus said: "Do not lie, and do not do what you hate, for all things are plain to Heaven. For there is nothing hidden that shall not become manifest, and there is nothing covered that shall not be revealed."

Jesus's disciples are requesting his advice, but he doesn't answer them directly. He wants them to discover life for themselves and exercise true human freedom.

The main thing, Jesus says, is be natural and do what you like. This is the meaning of "do not lie." Do things because you want to, not because you feel an obligation to do them. To do something you don't want because it is your duty is to lie to yourself. Most of us do this all the time. Or we do something with a view to making a profit. This egocentric way of thinking is blind to the Order of the Universe. Seeking physical, mental, or spiritual profit is another form of lying.

These ways of thinking and acting are dualistic. For example, a divided mind eats whole natural food to cure sickness, not because it is the appropriate food for human beings. When the sickness is overcome, the previous chaotic way of eating is resumed. Jesus is encouraging his students: Don't be conceptual. Don't think: Should I fast? Should I pray? Should I follow a certain diet? Don't feel "I should do this" or "I should do that." Wipe out "should," "must," and "ought." That mind is still struggling, comparing, competing.

The first stage of living in harmony with universal order is conceptual. We need some guidelines and limitations. But as our health and judgment improve, we naturally become more modest and humble. In the second stage, we automatically know what needs to be done. We become more intuitive and enjoy what we really want to do. We don't feel a mission or sense of responsibility. There is no concept of sacrifice or doing something for the sake of the world or society or family. Jesus is teaching people real freedom. If you don't want to do it, don't do it. Do it if you really enjoy it from the bottom of your heart. That is being truthful with yourself. Real freedom is light and gives us energy. It is play, not work or sacrifice.

7. Jesus said: "Blessed is the lion that the man devours and the lion will become human. Cursed is the man whom the lion devours and [the man will become lion]."

Jesus is not recommending that people eat large mammals. He is using this as an analogy to teach about biological and spiritual evolution. In the order of nature, human beings are higher than animals (*see* Figure 4). Our appropriate principal food is whole cereal grains, such as the whole grain barley bread that Jesus distributed to his followers. If we eat grains as the center of our meal, we become strong, healthy, peaceful, and evolve endlessly toward the world of spirit. But for us to eat a lion is to degenerate or go backward on the evolutionary spiral. From the lion's side, it is cause for blessings because it is the target of all animals eventually to become human.

Jesus may have taken his text from the story in the Bible about Daniel in the lion's den. Chapter 1 of the *Book of Daniel* relates that Daniel ate only grains and vegetables and on account of his diet was healthier and better nourished than all the other young men of his generation. When his enemies threw him into the lion's den, the lions wouldn't eat him because he was a real man. He ate all vegetable-quality foods. The lions could sense his vibration. If we eat mostly grains and vegetables, we will never be threatened by wild animals. Lions, tigers, and other creatures will not be attracted to us. Nor will insects.

Traditional people know very well that if you eat some sugar or a piece of watermelon you will get bitten by mosquitoes, but if you don't eat sweets or fruit they will leave you alone.

Figure 4. The Spiral of Evolution.

7. Primordial Life
6. Sea Moss
5. Sea Vegetables
4. Land Moss
3. Ancient Plants
2. Modern Plants, Fruit Trees
1. Grains

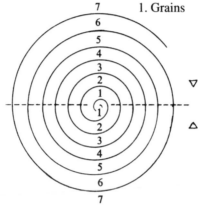

1. Human Beings
2. Mammals, Apes and Chimpanzees
3. Reptiles, Birds
4. Amphibians
5. Sea Vertebrates
6. Sea Invertebrates
7. Primordial Life

For an animal or insect to bite us, we must already have been eating very disharmoniously. To be consumed by a lion is to regress through millions of years of past biological evolution and be cursed, but we have only ourselves to blame. Evidently in Jesus's day, attacks by wild animals in the wilderness were common, indicating that many people were not eating in an orderly way. Today generally people are in worse shape than back then. We are attacked by viruses and bacteria—the lowest forms of life. In a healthy bloodstream, these tiny mircroorganisms cannot survive and pose no threat. However, if our blood and lymph quality have degenerated, they may secure a lethal foothold.

As we grow older, our consciousness should naturally get higher and higher and after death continue on in the next world. However, today we eat so much chicken, beef, milk, cheese, ice cream, and other animal food that we degenerate, bringing on untold sicknesses and difficulties, suffering in this world and the next. At another level, this passage teaches us that human beings are consumed by their dream. We are devoured or killed by our view of life. If our aim is riches and honors or some material end symbolized by the lion, we will eventually be eaten by our limitations. But if our dream is infinite—macrobiotics or the endless view of life—we will become one with God or the infinite universe and find and live with eternal life.

8. And he said: "The Man [who is Living] is like a wise fisherman who cast his net into the sea. He drew it up from the deep full of small fishes. Among them he found a big, marvelous fish. That wise fisherman, he threw all the small fishes back into the sea. He chose the big fish without hesitation. Whoever has ears to hear, let him hear."

What do the fish stand for? They are our desires, ambitions, or dreams: money, degrees, possessions, marriage, status, fame. There are many fishes in the sea. We want so many things out of life. What is the biggest fish—the greatest dream? That is finding God, the Infinite One. The foolish fisherman is satisfied with lesser fish. If we are wise we shall throw back all others to take that one—Life itself and the understanding of its infinite order.

9. Jesus said: "Behold, the sower went out, filled his hand [with seeds], and cast them. Some fell on the road where birds came and gathered them. Others fell on rock and did not take root in the soil and did not bear heads of grain. And others fell on thorns which choked the seeds, and the worms

ate them. And others fell on the good earth, and it produced good fruit. It yielded sixty per measure and one hundred twenty per measure."

This is a parable about spreading health, happiness, and peace. The seeds are the teachings of eternal truth. Seeds don't grow on the road, on rocky soil, or among thorns. They require good soil. The good earth stands for proper nourishment and a well-developed understanding of the universe and life. The good earth yields people with strong bodies, minds, and spirits who are capable of passing on an understanding of universal order from generation to generation. Other people are like rocks and thorns. Lacking proper nourishment, they are too hard and critical for the teachings to take root.

In ordinary, honest people—like his disciples and those whom Jesus refers to elsewhere as the salt of the earth—the teachings will grow and grow, eventually covering the whole world. This is the meaning of yielding good fruit. Rearing sixty per measure and one hundred twenty per measure signify a limitless quantity. From one grain, ten thousand grains grow. This is another traditional way of stating that the order of the universe is infinite expansion. The more we get, the more we must give away. Then the more we get in return, and so on until we become one with eternal life itself.

10. Jesus said: "I have cast fire upon the world, and behold, I kindle it until it is aflame."

This saying is echoed in the *Gospel of Luke* where Jesus says, "I have come to kindle a fire on earth, and how I wish it were already burning!" [12:49] What is the fire that Jesus preaches? It is not physical fire, such as the revolutionary fire sown by the Zealots, a movement of Jewish resistance fighters, who wanted to free their country from Roman political rule. The fire signifies the teachings of eternal truth that burn away old delusions and imbalanced ways of life. The fire is consciousness, truth, or spirit. It is this fire that Jesus wants to spread among people. But very few people have the energy or passion for eternal life. They are content with lesser things—smaller fish. But not until the whole world recognizes the Kingdom of Heaven can Jesus rest. He has truly set his sight on realizing an endless dream.

11. Jesus said: "This heaven will pass away and the one above it will pass away. The dead are not living and the living will not die. In the days when you consumed the dead, you made it alive. When you enter the Light, what will you do? On the day when you were one, you became two. But when you are two, what will you do?"

In this passage, Jesus is referring again to the Spiral of Life. According to traditional cosmology, God or One Infinity gives rise to seven heavens or levels of being (*see* Figure 5). "This heaven will pass away." This heaven is the earth. Our life here shall pass away upon death.

"And the one above it will pass away." After death, we all go to the next world. But that heaven shall also pass away as we

Figure 5. The Seven Heavens.

7th Heaven: One Infinity, God
6th Heaven: Polarization, Yin and Yang,
    beginning of the Relative World
5th Heaven: Energy and Vibration,
    beginning of the Phenomenal World
4th Heaven: Preatomic Particles, begin-
    ning of the Material World
3rd Heaven: World of Elements and
    Physical Nature
2nd Heaven: The Vegetable Kingdom,
    beginning of the Organic World
1st Heaven: The Animal Kingdom,
    culminating in Human Beings

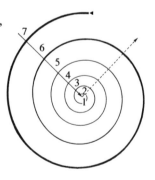

continue our journey to our infinite source. The planets, the stars, and the galaxies will ultimately perish and be left. "The dead are not living." The dead are things of the relative world, especially fragmentary, delusional ways of thinking. They shall all pass away in the worlds to come.

"And the living will not die." The living is the entire process of universal creation. Eternal order shall never die. It is the same here on earth as it is in heaven.

"In the days when you consumed the dead, you made it alive." When we were alive on this earth, we chased after many trifles such as riches and honors and followed many partial, fragmentary teachings. We consumed these lifeless objectives and dead doctrines and made them alive. They competed, struggled, and fought with one another. Our attachment to them gave them life and energy.

"When you enter the Light, what will you do?" In the world of energy and vibration, however, these fragmentary philosophies are useless. When we pass into the next world after death, these delusions are nothing.

"On the day when you were one, you became two." From One Infinity, in the far away past we differentiated into billions and came to the relative world, symbolized by two—plus and minus, centrifugal and centripetal force, expansion and contraction, male and female, brightness and darkness—comprehensively, yin and yang.

"But when you are two, what will you do?" Phenomena constantly appear and disappear. What shall we do in this life: Search out pleasure and comfort? Become rich and famous? Create something beautiful? Cultivate our intellect? Contribute to the development of society? Discover scientific truth? In the relative world, we are settling for ephemeral things as eternal life passes us by. If we are truly wise, we shall seek the absolute, invincible teaching that leads to discovery of our true self and live in the Kingdom of Heaven.

12. The disciples said to Jesus: "We know that you will de-

46

part from us. Who will lead us then?" Jesus said to them: "Wherever you are, you will go to James the Just for whose sake heaven and earth came into being."

James the Just is traditionally regarded as the brother of Jesus and the leader of the early Church in Jerusalem. According to Hegesippus, a second-century historian, "He [James] drank no wine or intoxicating liquor and ate no animal food . . . " In this passage, Jesus may be referring to his brother, but more likely he is simply encouraging his followers to go to any honest man. James was a very common name. Any place the disciples went they were bound to run into a just man. In Jesus's view, since everyone is a son or daughter of God or One Infinity, he can say that heaven and earth came into being for the sake of all.

13. Jesus said to his disciples: "Compare Me and tell Me whom I am like." Simon Peter said to him: "You are like a righteous angel." Matthew said to him: "You are like a wise philosopher." Thomas said to him: "Master, I am speechless to say whom you are like." Jesus said: "I am not thy Master, because you have drunk, you have become intoxicated from the bubbling spring which I have measured out." And he took him aside and said three words to him. Now when Thomas returned to his companions, they asked him: "What did Jesus say to you?" Thomas said to them: "If I tell you one of the words that he said to me, you will take up stones and throw them at me; and fire will issue from the stones and destroy you."

In this passage, as in the famous New Testament query "Who do men say that I am?," Jesus is testing his students' comprehension and understanding. His disciples compare him to an angel, sage, or other lofty being or like Thomas remain speechless.

The bubbling spring which Jesus has measured out—taught and warned against—is delusional knowledge. His followers are full of ephemeral wisdom. They are drunk on rituals, miracles, and signs and portents of historical prophecy. They are waiting for the return of Elijah and the Messiah to save them. Jesus is challenging them to discover the world of infinity from which they all originated and will all return and to take responsibility for their own salvation.

Thomas was very keen but kept missing the real essence of Jesus's teachings. Taking him aside, Jesus admonished him: "Thomas, wake up! Why are you so wishy-washy? Why don't you see the real you? Why don't you see the real me? We are one."

Then Jesus confided: "You are God—the Eternal One." Thomas was astonished. To the rest of the disciples, Jesus's teachings remained a mystery. Their level was still dualistic. They were smart in the relative world, but dumb in the truth. Later the Church they founded made Jesus a savior and made the people to be sinners. This was totally opposite to his teachings, but over the centuries millions of people died by fire or stoning for affirming their unity with the infinite source.

14. Jesus said to them: "If you fast, you will create sin for yourselves. If you pray, you will be condemned, and if you give alms, you will do violence to your spirits. And if you enter any land and wander the districts, and they receive you, eat what is set before you and heal the sick among them. For what goes into your mouth will not defile you, but what comes out of your mouth, that will defile you."

If divorced from an understanding of the infinite self, fasting, prayer, and giving alms are shameful. Jesus here is telling his followers not to degrade their spirit with penances. By trying to profit from these practices, they are only creating a greater separation between their ephemeral, changing desires—the little self or small i—and their eternal self—the Big I. Many spiritual practices can create barriers between people as can wealth or honors.

Jesus goes on to tell them how to eat and teach. Of course,

48

when they are with him they are all eating strictly macrobiotically—barley, whole grain bread, lentils, vegetables, and occasionally a little fish and fruit. Ordinarily they never eat meat,
poultry, dairy, sugar, or other extreme foods. This is why they
could heal many people. But now it is time to go out and spread
the teachings and visit village to village. People will give you
bad food, Jesus tells them. The way you handle this situation
will lead to opposition or agreement. Eat what is given. Eating
poor quality food once or twice won't hurt you. But if you reject
people and their food, you will lose their friendship and can't
help them. After you help relieve their sicknesses, then gradually they will change and follow your guidance in food and other
matters.

This is good advice today. Many young macrobiotic friends
are torn between following proper diet and pleasing their family
or friends. If they go home at Thanksgiving and Christmas and
reject their mother's cooking, they will not be able to help their
families. It is better to accept her food, chew well, and gradually
introduce her to a more healthy way of living.

**15. Jesus said: "When you see one who was not born of
woman, prostrate yourselves and worship him. That one is
your Father."**

The infinite universe is not born through sexual intercourse. That
is your Father—your source or origin. Do not worship, though
you may respect and be grateful to, phenomenal things such as
heros, prophets, and messiahs. Marvel at the endless wonder and
beauty of life as a whole.

**16. Jesus said: "Men may think that I have come to cast
peace upon the world. They do not know that I have come to
sow division upon the earth: fire, sword, war. For there shall
be five in a house: three against two and two against three,
the father against the son and the son against the father, and
they will stand as solitary ones."**

In this passage, Jesus is talking about the Five Transformations, one of the cornerstones of traditional teachings around the world (*see Saying* 19). In this "house"—the infinite universe—there are five basic energies: upward energy (symbolized by tree); active energy (fire); downward energy (soil, earth); gathering energy (metal, sword, war); and floating energy (water) (*see* Figure 6).

Figure 6. Five Trees in Paradise.

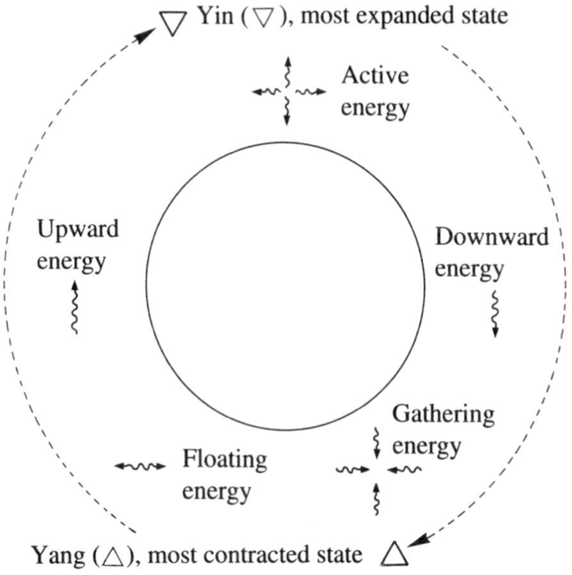

The five energies are mutually supportive and opposed. Depending on their position within the spiral, three energies are always aligned against two, and two are aligned against three (*see* Figure 7). In the *I Ching* or ancient Chinese *Book of Changes*, where the five transformations are more fully developed, family relationships are correlated with the five energies. The father and eldest son stand in natural conflict, as do the mother and eldest daughter, while the middle and youngest children are more in harmony with their parents. Jesus may be alluding to this natural order within the family.

Figure 7. I Ching Family Arrangement.

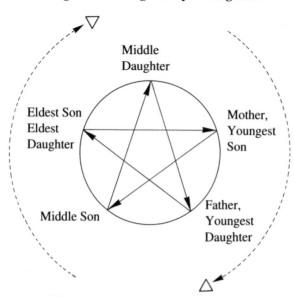

Jesus's teachings sow conflict because they differ so greatly from philosophy and religion as it was then practiced. Here he is telling his students that he has not come to make peace among the delusional and fragmented theories of the day. He has come to set the world on fire with a desire for eternal truth.

But in teaching people to take responsibility for their own destiny, families will inevitably be divided. Arguments will develop, separations will go. Father and son, mother and daughter, and brothers and sisters will be opposed. Some will return to a more natural way of life, eat well, marvel at the universe as a whole, and heal themselves. Despite natural antagonisms, as reflected in the five phases of transformation, they can stand as solitaries—i.e., act on behalf of One Infinity. Others will continue to eat bad food, lead an imbalanced life, and look to saviors, doctors, and miracle-workers. They will continue to suffer.

In the New Testament, Jesus says the same thing: "I came not to send peace but a sword." [*Matthew* 10:34] The divisions he

creates are natural ones, useful for a time until order and harmony can be restored in the world. The sword is the exercise of
higher judgment. He has come to reveal the sword of supreme
judgment leading to life everlasting that is everyone's birthright.

**17. Jesus said: "I will give you what no eye has seen and
what no ear has heard and what no hand has touched and
what no heart has known."**

In this saying, Jesus is talking about One Infinity and universal
being and its order. The universal Spiral of Life cannot be seen,
heard, or touched.

**18. The disciples said to Jesus: "Tell us how our end will be."
Jesus said: "Have you already discovered the beginning so
that you ask about the end? For where the beginning is,
there the end will be. Blessed is he who stands at the beginning, for he shall know the end and he shall not taste death."**

The disciples are still confused. After a few years, they are still
asking about their origin and destiny, their beginning and end.
They have not understood Jesus's teaching about the Big Self
and the little self—One Infinity and the infinitesimal. Jesus is
thinking: Why can't they understand? Why are they still asking?
In the *Book of Revelation* Jesus refers to himself several times
as "the Alpha and Omega, the beginning and the end." In several
parables in the Synoptic Gospels, he talks about the reversal of
order which takes place as the Spiral of Life unfolds. He also
talks about the wisdom of letting things happen without acting
as in the admonition to be like the birds of the air which sow not
or the lilies of the field that do not toil nor spin. [*Matthew* 6:26-
28] Jesus's teaching is very similar to the doctrine of non-action
found in India, China, Japan, and other countries of the East.
Nonaction means this: we should allow everyone and everything else around us to act fully, and by allowing that, we are
acting. We do not act by our own personal intention, but we act

by adapting to the actions of others or the surrounding environment. Secondly, we do not do certain special things with keen attention or attachment, because whatever has a beginning also has an end. If we act intentionally, our actions will have an end, and beginning and end become opposite—one is alpha or yin, the other is omega or yang. Whatever we do, the opposite results against our wish. So we can act, but we do not attach ourselves to our actions. Non-doing is the key to infinite freedom. By harmonizing ourselves with the endless order of change and embracing all apparent opposites—alpha and omega, life and death, health and sickness, peace and war, first and last—we shall stand at the beginning, know the end, and find eternal life.

19. Jesus said: "Blessed is he who was before he came into being. If you become disciples to Me and hearken to My words, these stones will minister to you. For [I say] to you there are Five Trees in Paradise, which remain unchanged in summer or in winter, and their leaves do not fall. Whoever knows them shall not taste death."

He who was "before he came into being" is One Infinity. These stones can teach you the Order of the Universe and guide you. Anything can teach and tell you what is life. Everything is a manifestation of universal order and reflects the dynamic interaction of yin and yang.

One gives rise to two. Two give rise to five. The Five Trees in Paradise are a poetic image used by Jesus to refer to a further differentiation of the everlasting, continuous manifestation of energy. In the East, this endless process was known as the Five Transformations. The electromagnetic energy or vibration generated between poles of outward and upward moving centrifugal (yin or alpha) force and inward and downward moving centripetal (yang or omega) force was classified into five basic types (*see* Figure 8).

1. *Upward Energy*: Light, upward movement arises and starts to become active.

Figure 8. Five Trees in Paradise: Daily and Seasonal Cycles.

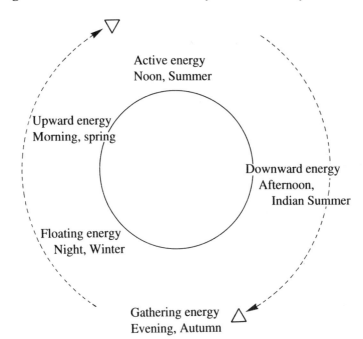

2. *Active Energy*: Expansion reaches a peak, diffusing actively in all directions.

3. *Downward Energy*: At its extreme, yin turns to yang and the contractive half of the cycle begins. Solidification or condensation begins.

4. *Gathering Energy*: The contractive tendency reaches its most compact, crystalized state. This tendency can be called gathering-like.

5. *Floating Energy*: At this stage, yang turns back to yin. Solidification starts to dissolve, and expansion arises.

Traditionally, the terms Tree, Fire, Soil, Metal, and Water were associated with the five transformations. However, they were used only to illustrate the transitory phases in this moving, dynamic process. They should not be taken literally.

It was understood that the energy within the human body and throughout nature flows in accord with this cycle. For example, atmospheric energy changes throughout the course of a day can be classified as follows:

1. *Morning*: the sun rises, the atmosphere expands, and the day's activities begin; expansive, upward energy.

2. *Noon:* the sun reaches a peak overhead and activity is at its height; diffuse, active energy.

3. *Afternoon*: the sun starts to reverse direction; activity diminishes; the atmosphere becomes heavier; downward energy.

4. *Evening*: the sun sinks and eventually sets; the atmosphere becomes more condensed; gathering energy.

5. *Night*: darkness prevails; the atmosphere feels suspended; melting or floating energy.

The seasons of the year can also be classified into five stages:

1. *Spring*: rising, expansive, upward energy.
2. *Summer*: very active, outward energy.
3. *Indian summer*: stabilized, falling, downward energy.
4. *Autumn*: solidified, gathering energy.
5. *Winter*: frozen, dissolving, floating energy.

There are countless other cycles within nature that reflect this universal order, including the origin and development of the universe and solar system, the rise of subatomic particles and elements, the biological evolution of plants and animals, the organs and systems of the body, the tastes and properties of foods, and personal and social character and destiny. The material form this process takes can be summarized as activating, plasmic, stabilizing, solidifying, and liquifying.

The flow of energy among the five stages of change exhibits two basic tendencies (*see* Figure 9). The first is nourishing or stimulating, and the second is antagonistic or conflicting. The nourishing tendency proceeds around the circle in a clockwise direction. Thus water nourishes wood or tree. Tree is burned into

Figure 9. Five Trees in Paradise: Complementary and Antagonistic Cycles.

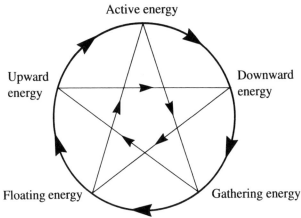

Outer clockwise direction=Nourishing cycle
Inner starlike direction=Complementary/antagonistic cycle

fire. Fire is reduced to ashes or soil. The soil hardens and turns into metal. Metal melts and becomes water.

The antagonistic tendency produces strain or conflict between every other stage. Thus tree roots hold the earth, controlling soil. Soil dams water. Water subdues fire. Fire melts metal. Metal chops down the tree.

The Five Transformations played a central part in many ancient cultures and civilizations. In Greece, it found expression in the Five Ages of Humanity (Gold, Silver, Copper, Bronze, and Iron) and found a counterpart in the doctrine of the Four Elements which formed the basis for traditional Western medicine from the time of Hippocrates until the Renaissance. (Sometimes a fifth element, Aether, was recognized along with Air, Water, Fire, and Earth.)

Five was a holy number in Judaism. The Torah consists of five books: *Genesis, Exodus, Leviticus, Numbers*, and *Deuteronomy*. (In turn, *Genesis* and other early scriptures like the *Psalms* are subdivided into five parts.) If we look at the form

Figure 10. Five Trees in Paradise: The Torah Cycle.

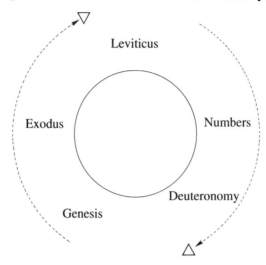

and content of these five books, we find that they unfold in an orderly way (*see* Figure 10). *Genesis*, the book of origins, is concerned with the separation of heavenly and earthly waters— that is, heaven and earth's force, yang and yin. It deals with seeds, new beginnings, and floods. Its quality is water. *Exodus* tells the story of the Jewish people's growth and development, their branching out. Its quality is tree. *Leviticus* concerns sacrifices, feasts, and festivals. Its very active quality is associated with fire. *Numbers* deals with wandering in the sandy desert and peaks and the development of priestly law and knowledge, judgment and discrimination in the promised land. Its quality is soil. *Deuteronomy* describes the development of modern urban society and the destruction and rebuilding of the Temple in Jerusalem. Its quality is condensed, integrating, metallic.

Everything follows this basic fivefold pattern of movement and rest, expansion and contraction, beginning and end. Whoever knows the universal laws of nature will enjoy eternal life. For Jesus, paradise is here and now. It is not located in heaven and the next life or in an ideal commonwealth on earth such as

Eden which once existed but which is now lost. Paradise here refers to the present universe.

To enter paradise is to understand the wonderful endless Order of the Universe in which we are always living, in this world and the next, and exercise our way of eating or using energy and vibration. Marveling at the fivefold dialectical laws of nature leads to true understanding and infinite health, happiness, and peace. The five trees of eternal life "remain unchanged in summer and in winter and their leaves do not fall." That means endless abundance can be ours.

Jesus is trying to get his disciples to see life from a much larger point of view. For them the leaves of the trees of paradise have all fallen. They can see only sickness, suffering, and misery around them. From a more modern view, everything appears to be random, chaotic, and unjust. But from the eye of God or One Infinity, there is no conflict or disequilibrium. All misfortune or sorrow that we experience is the result of our own ignorance or one-sided actions. Everything is proceeding in perfect harmony according to the spirallic laws and principles of the infinite universe.

The five trees are a dynamic compass to understand all aspects of life. In macrobiotic households around the world, families today are using this priceless treasure to harmonize with the seasons, cook, heal, travel, plan their homes, and understand personal, business, and social relationships.

20. The disciples said to Jesus: "Tell us what the Kingdom of Heaven is like." He said to them: "It is like a mustard seed, the smallest of all seeds. But when it falls on the tilled soil, it puts forth a large branch and becomes shelter for the birds of the air."

The Kingdom of Heaven is everything: the infinite universe itself and its supreme, invincible order. The Kingdom of Heaven is the total process of change. Out of this order comes the force that creates the phenomenal world, including galaxies, stars, planets, animals, plants, and human beings. That force is known by many names: yin and yang, alpha and omega, movement and rest.

Everything is born, grows, flourishes, and declines according to the laws of expansion and contraction. For example, like most living things, plants grow from seeds, which are very compacted or yang (*see* Figure 11). As the plant grows, it expands, becoming tall, and it opens up. This upward, outward growth is yin. In growing, the plant creates a flower and fruit. At this stage, it reaches its extreme yin form and begins to turn into its opposite. Inside the fruit, seeds are created, and they are very yang. As the plant declines, contracting in a more inward direction, it eventually withers and dies. But at the extreme yang stage of death, its seed takes root, and new life is born. So in this process, yang produces yin, yin produces yang, and so on continuously.

Figure 11. Five Trees in Paradise: Stages of Plant Growth.

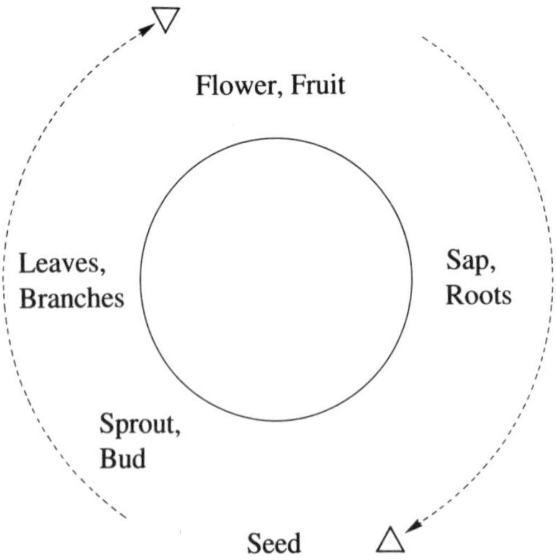

Flower, Fruit

Leaves,
Branches

Sap,
Roots

Sprout,
Bud

Seed

The Kingdom of Heaven governs everything, and without it no one or nothing exists. Everything has the same order, the same principle, whether material or spiritual, visible or invisible, human beings or matter, soul or spirit. Atoms, plants, animals, human beings, cultures and civilizations, star systems and galaxies—everything moves within the same order. That is the Kingdom of Heaven. It goes on forever and ever. It has no beginning and has no end. It is infinite and eternal. We may say that it is God or the law of God and is without beginning or end.

In using a mustard seed as an example, Jesus once again is trying to show that we can learn about this endless order from the most simple things. Everything is our teacher: seeds, stones, flowers, candles, leaven. The life of everything proceeds according to universal laws (see Appendix). Yin attracts yang, yang attracts yin. At their extremes, yin produces yang, yang produces yin. The greater the front, the greater the back. The first shall become last, the last shall become first.

From tiny, insignificant beginnings, great works and big dreams are realized. Nothing is impossible for someone who has the smallest faith in the Order of the Universe, for they know that the seed contains the harvest. From one grain, ten thousand grains grow. From ten thousand grains, ten million grains are produced. Infinite expansion is the law of the infinite universe. Everything unfolds *spirally* like a plant out of a seed.

21. Mary said to Jesus: "Whom are your disciples like?" He said: "They are like small children who have taken over a field which is not theirs. When the owners of the field come, they will say: 'Give back to us our field.' The children will take off their clothes in the presence of the owner and return the field to them. Therefore I say: If the head of the house knows that the thief is coming, he will remain vigilant before he comes and will not let him break into his home to carry off his goods. You must then watch for the world, gird up your loins with all your might lest the robbers find a way to take advantage of you, because they will find the weakness which you [least] expect. Let there be among you a person of wisdom. When the grain ripened, the reaper came in haste with his sickle in his hand and he harvested it. Whoever has ears to hear, let him hear."

The disciples are like naive children, playing around and chasing after vain, ephemeral things. The field which is not theirs is the small self. In it they have dressed themselves with illusions. The thief is the temptation to follow these delusions, whether of our own creation or of the society in which we live. Such impulses take us away from our real self. They sneak in the mind, confuse and spoil us, and make us forget that we are always one with infinity.

The delusions of our modern day society differ little from those in Jesus's time. They include seeking pleasure and comfort, riches and power, love and beauty, scientific truth and medical knowledge, social status and honors, and other relative ends. The brigands that can distract us from our true self—our lord—frequently come in the shape of desire for improper food, especially extreme yin such as sugar, honey, chocolate, milk, white flour, white rice, ice cream, candy bars, tofu cheesecake, and tropical vegetables and fruits. (Jesus cursed the fig tree because its fruits are too yin for ordinary consumption, even in a hot climate.) However, they can also come in the shape of extreme yang, such as meat, poultry, eggs, too much fish and seafood, and excessive salt, which contributes to a narrow, rigid mind and spirit.

Whoever thinks they can escape the consequences of improper behavior or eating better think twice. Jesus reminds them that they may reap sudden loss, sickness, or accident as a result of their own actions. They must discard their illusions—take off their clothes. They must be especially careful of trifling things like an unkind word or a rich dessert. Like the mustard seed, a false step can grow into a huge calamity. Cancer begins with the first helping of ice cream. Divorce starts from the first lover's quarrel. A person of understanding—someone who knows the laws of change and harmony—will not be tempted to quarrel or binge around. When he or she discovers the endless Order of the Universe, he immediately puts it into practice. He reaps the fruit of eternal life.

22. Jesus saw children who were being nursed. He said to his disciples: "These children who are giving suck are like those who enter the Kingdom." They said to him: "Shall we then, as children, enter the Kingdom?" Jesus said to them: "When you make the two one, and when you make the inner as the outer and the outer as the inner and the above as the below, and when you make the man and the woman into a single one, so that the man will not be male and the woman will not be female, when you make eyes in the place of an eye, and a hand in the place of a hand, and a foot in the place of a foot, and an image in the place of an image, then you shall enter [the Kingdom]."

In this and similar passages in the New Testament about little children, Jesus is not talking about becoming like a child. He is talking about yin and yang directly. The sucking baby is taking its mother's milk. That is the important thing, not that it is help-less and crying out. Mother and baby are one. A baby is very small, compact, yang. It is nourished by mother's milk, which is very abundant, expansive, yin. Yang baby and yin milk are united. Yin changes into yang. Yang changes into yin. Jesus is talking about the Order of the Universe being made here, not the baby's mind. Many people have misunderstood this teaching and taken Jesus's words to mean they should be infantile or childlike.

The disciples, who hold to this view, then ask whether they shall enter the Kingdom of Heaven. They are relatively un-spoiled, pure, trusting, and innocent. They are following Jesus around like little children waiting for him to save them like an angel come down from heaven. Jesus says: No, naive, childlike behavior is not enough to reach paradise. To enter the Kingdom they must know how to balance yin and yang, to harmonize, combine, and make order. Making "the two one" means under-standing how to harmonize and combine different and opposite things—yin and yang—producing one. The same is true about transforming yin outer into yang inner and yin above to yang below. Making "male and female into a single one" again means changing yang into yin and vice versa.

Making "eyes in the place of an eye," "hands in the place of a hand," "a foot in the place of a foot," and "an image in the place of an image" simply means to make order. Again Jesus is saying if you can arrange everything according to yin and yang, you are in the Kingdom of Heaven. You are living as a free person in this universe.

Unfortunately, the second part of this teaching about making order was left out of the New Testament and only the first part about the children was retained. Probably the editors, like the disciples here, couldn't understand it. Jesus's true teaching was lost, and the idea arose in the Church that the Kingdom is not a living, ever-present reality but something we enter after death. Fortunately, his original words have now been recovered after nearly two thousand years. In our macrobiotic cooking classes, we are freely changing yin into yang and yang into yin. When we prepare food, we learn to balance fire and water, salt and oil, liquid and solid, animal and vegetable quality, time and pressure. Our macrobiotic friends are truly beginning to live in the Kingdom of Heaven and extending order from their kitchens to all parts of society and the world as a whole.

23. Jesus said: "I shall choose you, one in a thousand, and two in ten thousand, and you shall stand as a solitary one."

The Order of the Universe is very simple. Every seed, leaf, stone, and drop of water demonstrates it. Yet we are adorned with so many delusions that we fail to see it. Very few, only one in a thousand or two in ten thousand, will really awaken to their eternal self. Those who do so will become representatives of One Infinity. Though they will still have different personalities and expressions, in essence they are one. They will stand united and teach eternal truths.

24. His disciples said: "Show us the place where you come

from, for it is necessary for us to seek it." He said to them: "Whoever has ears, let him hear. In a man of light, there is light, and he gives light to the whole world. If he does not shine, there is darkness."

The disciples again ask Jesus where he comes from. They marvel at his words and want to know his origin. The question, he tells them, is not one of geography. They are both living in the same place, in the Kingdom of Heaven. The difference between him and the disciples is that he has light, or understanding. By living as a manifestation of One Infinity, he is capable of transforming or lighting up the whole world. If a person doesn't manifest the light or act with understanding, they are acting in darkness. The light is not difficult to manifest once you discover it. In some people it is only a small light at first, in others it is big. Like everything else, it will grow and shine out through your behavior, your words, and your day to day life. But it can also be dimmed or go out, especially if you eat excessively unhealthy foods or desserts.

25. Jesus said: "Love your brother as your soul, guard him as the apple of your eye."

Helping others is easy to understand, but difficult to do. Unless you have confidence of oneness with the Order of the Universe, you cannot develop this spirit. Now AIDS is spreading around the world. Who's responsible: The gay community? Haitians, Africans, and other people from the tropics? Television and movies? The pharmaceutical industry and medical profession? The food processing industry?

Of course, most modern institutions are behaving very fruitlessly in the face of this crisis. But they are not responsible for creating it. You and I are responsible. Don't distribute responsibility to others. Don't think because there are five billion people in the world, you are only one five billionth responsible. No, we must take 100 percent responsibility for the world in which we live. The same thing with war, cancer, and family decline. We must really feel it and develop a sense of oneness with others and understand what they are thinking and feeling. More and more, as we understand the Order of the Universe and our light grows, we can practice helping others. We can really care for and love others, not minding to throw our life away for their happiness.

Modern society is very egocentric, maybe even more than in Jesus's day. In his time, there were big divisions between people and cultures. In our day, prejudice and discrimination continue, but today many people hesitate to help even their own family, children, wife or husband. They think: "Why are they suffering? It's not my business. God is punishing them with AIDS or cancer." This is a selfish, arrogant view. This mind can't see life, understand our infinite origin or destiny, and enter the Kingdom of Heaven. Such people never find the light. It is very sad. They remain confused, always suffering. They pass blindly through their life, from darkness to darkness. Inevitably they will suffer and perish. We must be one with them, help them see the reality of oneness. Through our quiet, patient love and care, especially proper food and clean natural environment, they may awaken.

26. Jesus said: "You see the mote that is in your brother's eye, but you do not see the beam that is in your own eye. When you cast the beam out of your eye, then you will see clearly to cast the mote out of your brother's eye."

It is easy to see the defects of other people and to criticize and complain. But it is difficult to see our own. What is the biggest defect? Arrogance—or ignorance of ourselves, ignorance of our life, why we came here, and where we are going. If we can see ourselves, we can see everyone and guide them. We cannot really heal anyone until we first heal ourselves. For that, we need to study the infinite universe and its laws. The principles of yin and yang and the five transformations are wonderful tools for diagnosing ourselves and other people. Once we discover our own mistakes and shortcomings, we can make self-reflection, adjust our way of eating and living to bring us into greater balance, and let our light spread to other people.

27. [Jesus said:] "If you do not fast from the world, you will not find the Kingdom. If you do not keep the Sabbath as the Sabbath, you will not see the Father."

The world Jesus is talking about here is the ordinary, everyday world of contemporary business, government, and family affairs. He is not talking about life on earth as such or recommending asceticism. The ordinary, everyday world in his day, as in ours, is a world of various delusions. Dualistic thinking is everywhere, dividing people into black and white, friend and foe, the saved and the damned, the educated and uneducated, rich and poor. Institutions that are supposed to support human growth and development such as the educational system, medicine, science, and religion are spreading delusions and on many occasions contributing to disorder. In order to find the one infinite life, we have to overcome or abstain—fast—from systems and conventional ways of looking at the world based on ignorance or partial understandings of reality.

What is the Sabbath? All around the world, people are keeping a holy day once a week. Jews observe Saturday, Christians observe Sunday, Moslems observe Friday. Does Sabbath mean going to synogogue, church, or mosque once a week and observing a day of rest? No, this is not the Sabbath. This is social custom. Sabbath means seventh day. But it does not signify a twenty-four hour day.

Sabbath is the seventh heaven or level of creation. On the Spiral of Life, the other six stages are moving relatively (*see* Figure 12). The seventh stage—God or One Infinity—is the origin of all origin. It is the highest level. It is at rest. It is the absolute world out of which the other six worlds appear.

Observing the Sabbath means to return to the realm of infinity. It involves cleaning out from the mind and heart the

Figure 12. The Sabbath or Seventh Heaven.

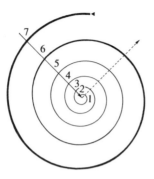

7. Sabbath
   God
   One Infinity
6. Polarization
5. World of Vibration
4. Preatomic Particles
3. World of Elements
2. Vegetable Kingdom
1. Animal Kingdom

The space outside of the spiral is the unmanifested absolute world of rest, and the worlds within the spiral are the moving relative and ephemeral worlds.

delusions of the world and recalling back to our eternal origin and source. To observe the Sabbath is to forget all wishy-washy activities. Whether we work, go to the cinema, or drive an automobile is immaterial. Historically, the original meaning of Sabbath was forgotten, and it became formalized as a day of rest during which certain activities such as these were avoided. It is not a day of rest but a day of awakening or reawakening.

Thousands of books have been written on theology. Thousands of sermons have been preached. Thousands of rules of conduct for observing the Sabbath have been formulated in different cultures. All of these are relative. The only important thing is One Infinity and you who have manifested out of it. You don't need any book, priest, or code to exercise love and help people. Every day can be the Sabbath. But at least once a week, once a month, or as often as you can, return to your source and origin by eating very simply—for example, just whole grain and a small portion of vegetables—meditate, pray, chant, take a walk in the woods, or do anything you like that helps bring you back to your true self. If you observe every day as the Sabbath, you will become a man or woman of light and help many people.

**28. Jesus said: "I took my place in the middle of the world
and I appeared to them in flesh. I found them all intoxicated.
None of them was athirst. And my soul was troubled for the
children of men, because they are blind in their heart and do
not see that they came into the world empty and they seek to
depart the world again empty. But now they are drunk.
When they have shaken off their wine, they will then repent."**

Jesus is talking again about delusions and the fascination that the
ephemeral world exerts on people. He tells his students that he
came here from One Infinity and was born to reveal eternal
truths. But he found everyone intoxicated—drunk—with delusions, wishy-washy views, superstitions, isms, and doctrines. No
one is athirst for knowledge of their real self. Everyone is chasing after empty—or ephemeral—pleasures and knowledge.
Some people will be shocked when cancer comes, when their
treasure is taken, or when their family has an accident and dies.
Then when the wine of the passing world wears off, they may
realize what is really important in life and wake up.

The word "repent" (*metanoia* in the Greek) originally meant
to turn away or reverse course. To repent means to change direction from yin to yang or from yang to yin. It has nothing to do
with sin, guilt, or confession. It has to do with freely using the
universal energies around us, especially those in our daily food,
to bring us back into harmony with the Eternal Universe and its
order.

**29. Jesus said: "If the flesh has come into being because of
the spirit, it is a marvel. But if the spirit has come into being
because of the body, it is a marvel of marvels. But I marvel
at how this great wealth has made its home in this poverty."**

In this verse, Jesus is explaining the Spiral of Life (*see* Figure
13). From the Seventh Heaven, or Sabbath, we journey through
six stages of creation in a downward, inward moving direction.

Figure 13. The Spiral of Physicalization and Spiritualization.

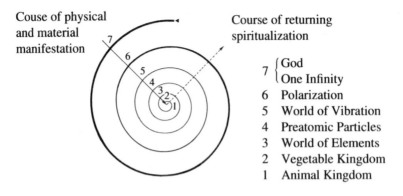

Couse of physical and material manifestation

Course of returning spiritualization

7 { God / One Infinity
6 Polarization
5 World of Vibration
4 Preatomic Particles
3 World of Elements
2 Vegetable Kingdom
1 Animal Kingdom

This is the spiral of physicalization. After manifesting on this earth, we start to go back in the other direction, moving in an upward, outward direction. This is the spiral of spiritualization.

"This great wealth" is One Infinity or our big self. "This poverty" is our small self. What Jesus is saying is that our body, that flower, this stone, and everything else in the relative world is a manifestation of the Eternal and its endless Order.

He is amazingly clear. Many people think the body is not important or that food is not important. They seek only the soul. But Jesus knows the true relationship. He says it is a marvel that our body has come into existence because of the infinite spirit. But it is even more marvelous that the infinite spirit has come into existence because of the body. He marvels most of all because the infinite has made its home in the infinitesimal. Through proper care of the body, through proper food selection and cooking, and through proper care of the natural world around us, we make our way back to the spiritual world.

When we eat brown rice or other whole grains as our basic food, we naturally begin to marvel at the world around us. Our mind becomes clear, flexible, and open to other people and the surrounding environment. We do not feel that we know everything. Like a child, we marvel at the world around us.

Closely related to a sense of marvel is humility. Humility is praise of the Order of the Universe. "Oh how wonderful this world is!" "How marvelous is God's creation!" "How beautiful the sky is!" Humility is praise—awe and constant praise of the infinite order around us of which we are a tiny part. Humility is not bending over, bowing with your head down, or praying—although that is also fine. The universal meaning of humbleness is constant praise of everything.

When you cut vegetables, be amazed at the beauty of those vegetables. When you eat a slice of apple, be amazed at how juicy, sweet, and beautiful it is. Think how was this made? Marvel at the same order running through everything. Praise the Order of the Universe and the long, long journey you have gone through.

In the Far East, this sense of wonder is also called beginner's mind. To praise everything is to have a beginner's mind. Everything you see is beautiful. Everything you see is wonderful. You are just like a child who awakes and starts to see the wonders of the world for the first time. A car is wonderful. The sky is wonderful. An airplane flying is wonderful. The radio is wonderful. That wonder, that praise is a beginner's mind. Everywhere you find the Order of the Universe, God, the Kingdom of Heaven. For the beginner's mind, there is nothing that is bad. Everything is marvelous.

Jesus has a burning spirit inside of him to help others and awaken them to the infinite life. If you know only this one verse, you and Jesus are one.

30. Jesus said: "Where there are three gods, they are gods. Where there are two or one, I am with him."

The expression in this verse is a little yang—short, abrupt, condensed. It is not so easy to understand unless we are eating well and our intuition is sharp.

Once again, Jesus is talking about the relation between the relative and absolute worlds. "Three gods" refers to the worlds of multiplicity—heavens one through five (*see* Figure 5)."Two

or one" refers to the last two heaven—heavens six and seven.
What Jesus means is that he is not attached to the relative world.
Three gods are still just gods, subject to higher laws. Jesus is to
be found with those higher laws—the two or the one—which are
the origin of everything. Jesus is always acting as the representative of the two—yin and yang—and the one—One Infinity.

**31. Jesus said: "No prophet is honored in his own village, no
physician heals those who know him."**

Our advice won't work with parents. Many young macrobiotic
friends have experienced this when they go home and talk to
their families about health and diet. They never listen. They
can't be objective or detached. They remember when you were
in diapers. By the same token, it's very hard for parents to help
their own child. Other children are very easy to help. There are
so many past circumstances there that parents can't be objective.
They have known you since birth. They know your old nature
and all your faults. They don't think you have any special understanding or ability. The same with your old friends. They know
your defects. It is very hard for them to listen, even though they
would benefit from your advice.

In terms of yin and yang, this verse illustrates the universal
law that likes repel and opposites attract (*see* the Appendix).
Members of the same family tend to repel each other, while
strangers are attracted. It also reminds us that everything has
both front and back, or a visible and invisible side; and the bigger the front, the bigger the back. You see only the marvelous
Order of the Universe you have recently discovered and want to
share with your parents. They see only the old disorderly you.
You see the mountain, your friends see the molehill. You see
great wealth, they see great poverty. You see One Infinity, they
see the infinitesimal. It's really very amusing, isn't it? Wonderful teachings are always accompanied by wonderful inability to
see or hear.

It takes time to help your parents or friends. But if you can change your mother and father, you are a real teacher. Jesus had a great deal of difficulty with his family. (*see Verses* #16, 55, 99, and 105 below.) Buddha changed his parents after many years. One day his father and retainers came and listened to him speak about the Wheel of the Wonderful Law (i.e., the Spiral of Life and the Order of the Universe). His father became his disciple.

My greatest happiness was to change my parents. After I graduated from Tokyo University, my parents hoped I would go into banking, government, law, or business. Instead I went to America to spread macrobiotics. On Fifth Avenue, I sat on the steps of St. Patrick's Cathedral in New York watching thousands of people pass by to understand why some people were healthy and happy and other people with sick and unhappy. Slowly I began to understand the marvelous Order of the Universe. Meanwhile, I worked as a bell boy, washed dishes, and had other odd jobs. Fifteen years later, in Boston, I was still struggling to make ends meet. My wife, Aveline, and I started teaching from our home and spent evenings pouring tamari soy sauce from a big jar into little jars for our students. About this time my parents came over from Japan to visit me for the first time. They spent two weeks listening to my lectures to a handful of people and watching me pour tamari soy sauce. One night they came and said they would like to talk to me in their room. I was afraid they would ask me to return to Japan. Instead they told me that what I was doing was really wonderful. They said they wanted to be my disciples.

I was the happiest person in the whole world. I was crying in my heart. How wonderful parents are! They gave me the highest education. What I was doing had no economic value, but they saw its real value. I was released at that moment from my ordinary family relationship with them. We were no longer parents and child. Later, I visited Japan and three hundred relatives became macrobiotic and my students.

If your parents become your disciples, you can change thousands of people. It doesn't matter in life how much money you make or what job you have. What matters is that you give your dream to the next generation. If you have a big dream, it will continue for thousands and thousands of generations and never perish. Jesus's dream is still continuing two thousand years later. That's because his dream is everyone's dream. Everyone wants life, health, happiness, truth, peace.

32. Jesus said: "A city that is built on a high mountain and fortified cannot fall, nor can it be concealed."

The high mountain is an understanding of the Order of the Universe. The city is our life or dream. There are many levels of understanding and expression in the relative world. If you talk as a politician, a businessman, or as a parent or child, your influence will remain limited. But if you talk and act from the highest place—One Infinity and its Endless Order—everyone can benefit. By building your life on faith in the Order of the Universe, your understanding will continuously grow and become a beacon to others.

33. Jesus said: "What you hear in one ear and in the other ear, preach from your housetops. For no one lights a lamp and puts it under a bushel, nor does he put it in a secret place, but he sets it on the lampstand, so that all who enter and leave may see its light."

This verse is closely connected to the last one. Jesus is telling his disciples to endlessly distribute his teachings of eternal truth. They should put their light in the highest place, the level of One Infinity. If they preach from there, they will illuminate everything and tower over all special interests and concerns.

34. Jesus said: "If a blind man leads a blind man, they shall both fall into the ditch."

A blind man is someone who doesn't see One Infinity or its marvelous order. If he or she leads others, they both will suffer.

There are many professional blind men today, as there were in Jesus's time, including many doctors, lawyers, scholars, politicians, and intellectuals. They can't heal themselves, so how can they possibly heal others? Be careful of people spreading disorder in the name of order. Find a person of understanding to study with or manifest your own light.

35. Jesus said: "It is not possible for one to enter the house of the strong man and take him by force unless he ties his hands. Then he will plunder his house."

The strong man is someone who understands and has faith in the Order of the Universe. The house is their mind, consciousness, and world around them. They could be a king, businessman, lawyer, taxi driver, housewife, or anyone with a strong view of life and confidence in eternal order.

Their confidence cannot be shaken by force or material loss or gain. Even in jail they can think clearly. But if you can bind their hands—cause them to lose their understanding of the order of the infinite universe—yin and yang—you can destroy their freedom.

Consciousness is always accompanied by action. They are two sides of the same coin. If we are a person of light, our actions shine with that light. We act from that oneness and unity. If our understanding remains just conceptual, we are not really free. To bind a free man's actions, you have to bind his or her consciousness.

What is the easiest way to penetrate and enter the house of consciousness? To develop your consciousness, you have to eat nourishing, well-balanced food. If you don't eat well, your consciousness collapses. Excessive intake of meat, sugar, eggs, ice cream, dairy food, and other improper items can cause us to forget who we are entirely. The most powerful way of altering consciousness is through food. The Jewish people had a mighty kingdom, but it was destroyed and scattered because they forgot the simple traditional and nourishing way of eating of Abraham,

Moses, and their ancestors. From Isaiah to Jesus, the prophets kept urging them to return to simple food, mostly grains and vegetables, but they did not understand. They could only go part way. Their food code represented a compromise between the traditional way of eating and the modern way of eating, dependent on animal food, imports, and unseasonal cooking. But thanks to keeping kosher food laws for thousands of years, the Jewish people were able to hold to the image of God and not completely perish.

The same thing is happening all around the world today. In Japan, hamburgers, soft drinks, and other modern foods have become very popular. On the one hand, they are very convenient and give rich sensory satisfaction. On the other hand, they tend to lead to sickness and weakened judgment. As a result, the Japanese people are losing respect for their parents and ancestors. Their traditions are crumbling. The same thing is happening in the United States and Europe. Just sixty years ago, parents and grandparents were observing a different way of eating. They ate many more whole grains, unrefined bread, fresh vegetables, and other unprocessed foods. They had more consciousness of God and of family, relatives, ancestors, and their community.

In East and West, North and South, an understanding of infinite order has been lost. Nearly everyone is sick, unhappy, and confused. Cancer, heart disease, AIDS, mental illness, infertility, family decline, crime, and war are widespread. Modern technology and medicine, government and education, are powerless to stop their spread. The only solution they can see is artificial and symptomatic: organ transplants, test tube births, behavior modification drugs, and other intervention into human biological systems in addition, of course, to bigger and better hospitals, jails, and armies.

Natural human biological and spiritual evolution is at stake. The root cause for our present crisis is that our understanding and application of universal order has been lost. Individuals, families, and cultures have forgotten how to balance food and environment for health, happiness, and peace. Humanity's hands have been bound by the spread of unnatural food and massive artificial agriculture, and our planet is being ransacked. We must awaken before it is too late.

36. Jesus said: "Take no heed from morning until evening and from evening until morning for what you wear."

What we put on every day are not only clothes. We also put on ideas, concepts, doctrines, titles, awards, achievements, grades. They are ephemeral and changing. Like fashions, they last a season, a year, or sometimes an era, but sooner or later they go out of style and are forgotten. Ancient Israel vanished away, the Roman Empire collapsed, and someday America, the Soviet Union, and modern civilizations will also disappear. Jesus is warning us here not to think about lesser, ephemeral things. People's reputation or their evaluation of others is superficial. Social, cultural, and national standards will all pass away. But you are a manifestation of One Infinity, the unchanging one. Act from that place and play with eternal life.

37. His disciples said: "When will you be revealed to us and when will we see you?" Jesus said: "When you take off your clothing without feeling ashamed, and take your garments and like small children place them on the ground and trample them underfoot, then [you will see] the Son of the Living One, and you will not be afraid."

The disciples are asking where Jesus is coming from. After he speaks, they are astonished. They speculate that he is the long awaited Messiah, who will reveal himself to the accompaniment of celestial trumpets, angels, and the destruction of their enemies.

It is this view of deliverance that Jesus is trying to dispell. In this verse like the last one, clothing and outer garments represent the delusional beliefs and attitudes people live by most of the time. Jesus tells his disciples that if they strip themselves of their

76

illusions and lesser concerns and be natural like children playing dress-up and who are not attached to the clothes—or superficial matters—they wear, they will regain their freedom and spontaneity. They will awaken to their true identity as sons and daughters of the Living God and have no fear. They will see themselves and Jesus as one. They will not seek after messiahs and saviors but take charge of their own destiny.

38. Jesus said: "Many times have you longed to hear these words that I say to you, and you have no one else to hear them from. There will be days when you will look for Me and you will not find Me."

In this verse, Jesus is scolding his students and telling them how dumb they are. The disciples are all seeking truth—knowledge of their imperishable, permanent, real self (Me). But no one could explain it to them. I can tell you, Jesus says, but you don't understand. You are chasing after ephemeral things, and there is no one else to teach you what your heart knows to be true. I will not always be here, so take advantage of this opportunity while you can and become a person of light and understanding.

39. Jesus said: "The Pharisees and Scribes have been given the keys of knowledge and hidden them. Neither did they enter nor let those enter who wanted to. But you, be wise as serpents and innocent as doves."

In Jesus's day, the Pharisees and Scribes controlled day-to-day life. They inherited the keys to past wisdom. They are the custodians of the scriptures, the sacred architecture, the festivals, and other social and cultural institutions based on a deep understanding of the Order of the Universe.

Here Jesus is telling his disciples that the authorities know many things, but they hide them and don't really make people healthy, happy, and peaceful. They do not show people how to live as the Infinite One. They no longer teach about the infinite

Order of the Universe and its eternal law of change—namely, yin and yang and the five phases of transformation. They turn against anyone who tries to live as a free person.

But they can master and apply yin and yang—heaven's downward force that makes the snakes crawl and produces a rational intellect and earth's upward force that makes the birds fly and creates a gentle, trusting nature—and enter the Kingdom of Heaven. They can be balanced, whole, and free.

The Pharisees and Scribes of our own day are scholars, scientists, doctors, and lawyers. They are powerless to solve any of the essential problems of human destiny in modern civilization, from the common cold to cancer, from family quarrels to nuclear war. And like their predecessors, they actively prevent anyone who has the keys from using them. People today who don't submit to artificial regulations such as those related to citizenship, international travel, social codes, and health prevention, including unnecessary—and sometimes dangerous—restraints on their health or freedom, are locked up and declared an enemy of society.

40. Jesus said: "A grapevine has been planted without the Father and, as it has not taken root, it will be pulled up and be destroyed."

The vine is modern civilization. Here Jesus is saying that all teachings, doctrines, schools, views, and pursuits that are not based on an understanding of One Infinity and its Order are in vain. Their blossoming is only temporary. They will all perish away, while true teachings that are rooted in universal order will endure.

41. Jesus said: "He who has in his hand, to him shall be given; and he who does not have, from him even the little which he has shall be taken."

Some people think that life is unfair. The rich appear to get richer and the poor appear to get poorer. But Jesus is not looking at giving and receiving only in terms of material or monetary gain. He is saying that if you have the understanding of One Infinity in hand, you will enjoy health, happiness, peace, and freedom. You will receive more and more as your understanding grows. But if you lack understanding of the Order of the Universe, you will suffer sickness, accidents, and difficulties and possibly even lose your life.

The spiritual world, the world of our developing consciousness, is the world of expansion (*see* Figure 2). The world of physicalization is the world of contraction. At the stage of existence we are at now, it is much better to give than to receive. Giving out helps us become more and more highly developed and to become lighter and lighter until at last we reach universal consciousness and Supreme Judgment and become one with eternal life as a whole. Now if we receive something, and then we give that away, we have not become lighter. We have only maintained our present condition. In order to become lighter, we have to give away more than we receive. The most valuable thing we have to give away is our life and our eternal dream— that is, practically, giving our life for everyone's health, freedom, and happiness, and the peace of the world.

In the Sermon on the Mount, Jesus declared, "Blessed are the poor in spirit: for theirs is the Kingdom of God." [*Matthew* 5:3] Jesus taught people to become poor. To the materially rich young man, he advised, "If thou wilt be perfect, go and sell that thou hast, and give to the poor, and thou shalt have treasures in heaven: and come and follow me." [*Matthew* 19:21] Poverty is the origin of wealth—whether material wealth or spiritual wealth. To give away everything is actually much easier than to acquire great success. It's very hard to get fame, to earn degrees, to reach high position, to become rich. You must use many techniques, tell many lies, push yourself, and engage in fierce competition.

But Jesus's way—to give away everything—is the easiest way, though to many who have an egocentric view, it is the most difficult. In this he was not teaching sentimentality. He was making use of the principles and laws of the infinite universe (*see* the Appendix). Yin attracts yang, yang attracts yin; and at their extremes, yin produces yang, and yang produces yin. Jesus taught that by emptying yourself you can make yourself full. By becoming a vacuum, you can attract everything you really need. Then you are able to shine, just like the sun. Then you start to give away your spirit, your idea, your understanding, your dream. Jesus was like that. He trained himself to be a vacuum. That is why, still now, he continues to shine after two thousand years. Meanwhile, all who tried to become full disappeared. No one knows them. Their names and works died eternally, while Jesus has lived long centuries and his teachings will live forever. A very interesting secret of life is there.

42. Jesus said: "Be passers-by."

We are all travelers from infinity, to infinity, within infinity. We all come from the same place and will all return to our eternal home together. During our brief life here, the scenery is constantly changing. We too are changing as we experience endless change in the world around us. Nothing stays in one place.

Jesus is encouraging us to become travelers of life. He is saying, don't be attached to things of the relative world. Don't stagnate or be stubborn. Enjoy life as it changes day to day. Sometimes it will go up, other times down. Recognize that sickness precedes health, unhappiness leads to happiness, and order follows disorder.

Pass through this life lightly, peacefully. Don't get stuck. Don't become stubborn and kill and injure for property, honors, doctrines, or ephemeral gain. For example, should I buy a house? Yes, of course, that is a natural human need. But don't try to protect your house for the next thousand years. Don't build it at the cost of hurting other people or the environment. Don't sacrifice everything to protect your children and lose sight of the Infinite One. Remember, you can't take your house to the

next world. You can't control your children or grandchildren's
lives. How many young people have been spoiled by sentimental
parents shielding them from all suffering, difficulties, and unhappiness? Attachment—to security, wealth, love, even truth—
produces just the opposite of what you intend.

If you have a small capacity for giving, you will gather small
things in your life. If you have a large capacity, many people, a
lot of money, or other things may come to you. It's all right to
have millions of dollars, a grand house, and other possessions.
But let others enjoy them besides yourself. Even after you die,
people continuously enjoy them. Don't be attached. Always,
endlessly give and do things for others. Let them enjoy together
with you. Let your consciousness continue to travel freely
through all levels of existence with the spirit of "one grain, ten
thousand grains."

**43. His disciples said to him: "Who are you to say these
things to us?" [Jesus said to them:] "You know not who I
am, from what I say to you. For you have become like the
Jews who love the tree and hate the fruit and love the fruit
and hate the tree."**

Jesus's disciples cannot understand where he is speaking from
because of their attachments to this relative world. Some of
them are influenced by the theology and interpretations of the
Scribes and Pharisees. Others are guided by the revolutionary
spirit of the Zealots or by the ascetic practices of the Essenes.

Jesus is not talking just about Jewish people, but all contemporary modern people. He is just using them as an example. We
may instead say Americans or modern people in general. Jesus
is chiding his disciples. He is telling them they are no different
from most ordinary people who like some things and reject others:

> "I like my friends and hate my enemies."
> "I like light and hate the darkness."
> "I like happiness and hate unhappiness."

"I like wealth and hate poverty."
"I like beauty and hate ugliness."
"I like capitalism and hate socialism."

All these complemental things are manifestations of universal order, endlessly balancing, harmonizing, and complementing each other. Without darkness, there is no light. If cold is not present, there can be no warmth. Beauty depends upon ugliness. If capitalism arises, socialism comes out to make balance. We have to see life from the view of One Infinity. Everything is a manifestation of the spirallic movement of yin and yang. There is no absolute good or bad in the Infinite Universe. Energy goes up and down, moves in and out, spirals from periphery to center and then back to the periphery. One thing changes into another. Sickness changes into health. War changes into peace. But many people don't see this. They become attached to one thing and reject its complementary opposite. This is the meaning of "loving the tree and hating the fruit" and "loving the fruit and hating the tree." We love certain foods but not the atherosclerotic and cancerous condition they lead to. We hate crime but carry a ring full of keys.

In *Genesis*, this dualistic view was represented by the Tree of the Knowledge of Good and Evil. By eating from this tree instead of the Tree of Life (One Infinity), Adam and Eve grew attached to the phenomenal world—the world of "this and that." Their thinking became one-sided. They covered up their nakedness—sense of marvel or beginner's mind—with illusory concepts, doctrines, theories, and other "clothing."

Jesus is telling us not to think this is right and that is bad. Or this person is an enemy, that one is a friend. Everyone has merit. Everyone is a friend. Enemies can make us strong. An enemy is our true friend and teacher. Difficulty is the mother of becoming wise and happy. Poverty is the father of comfort and wealth. If we deny or reject one, taking another, we are dualistic and will become unhappy.

44. Jesus said: "He who blasphemes against the Father shall

be forgiven. He who blasphemes against the Son shall be forgiven. But he who blasphemes against the Holy Spirit shall not be forgiven either on earth or in heaven.''

The Father is this infinite universe—the invincible, absolute, eternal process of change. The central meaning of blaspheme is not to curse but to ignore or forget. If we forget or deny the existence of God, One Infinity, or heaven, we can still become healthy and happy. If we say, "I don't believe in God," we are forgiven.

The Son is this earth and the physicalized, materialized things upon the earth, including ourselves. The Son includes Jesus, as a teacher of eternal truth, but also every person. It also could be a stone, a mountain, a tree, you or me. If you say, "I hate that tree" or "I don't like him," it's still permissible, and you are forgiven. We all tend to like some things and dislike others. This is common attraction or repulsion in the course of natural process.

The Holy Spirit or Holy Ghost is the order permanently governing, ruling, or controlling the phenomenal world. It is the natural electromagnetic energy flowing between heaven and earth. In the ancient Middle East, it was known as *rauch*, a Hebrew word meaning "breath" or "spirit." In the Far East it was called *ki* or *chi* and in India *prana*.

The Holy Spirit should be interpreted as the working of invisible vibrations or laws (*see* Figure 14). Our life is governed by

Figure 14. The Eternal Process of Change: Jesus's View.

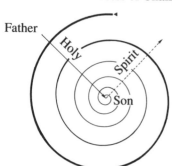

yin—centrifugal and expanding force—and yang—centripetal and contracting force. We are constantly bathed in a stream of natural electromagnetic energy and vibrations coming from heaven and earth. This energy enters the meridians and chakras of the body, stimulating all of our systems, as well as nourishing the brain and body cells. If we ignore this wonderful ordering mechanism—how this life has come out and how this life disappears, how this entire universe is going on, in our terms, yin and yang—that will never be forgiven in heaven or on earth.

Every day we are seeing examples of this. If you ignore, abuse, or violate the changing natural law of the universe, then you will experience immediate suffering. For instance, if you take excessive simple sugar, the next day you will experience a headache—suffering comes. If you take excessive liquid, then the next day you will have swelling or cloudiness in thinking or diarrhea. The effect appears proportionately to the cause. If you are not keeping a clear mind, you have an accident and difficulty. From these processes of cause and effect of the Order of the Universe, no one can escape—even if he is a billionaire, a president or king, a saint or wise man, or a beggar. This order is working very precisely, very accurately. Without exception, anyone who ignores or violates this order suffers because yin and yang are working everywhere. The Holy Spirit or the Order of the Universe is constantly processing all around and within us. The laws of dynamic movement govern this world, the next world, and other planets. You will not be forgiven. You will be troubled everywhere—until you awaken to the laws of order and harmony and change your way of thinking, eating, or living.

The same cosmology is found not only in Jesus's teaching but in Buddhism (*see* Figure 15). Buddhism talks about the Buddha, the Monk, and the Law. It is the same idea as the Father, Son, and Holy Ghost. The Buddha is a symbolic expression of the infinite universe. Instead of Son, they say the Monk. Monk stands for an individual manifestation of infinity, including a person who seeks the truth. The Law is the law of life or the Order of the Universe. For example, in Zen, it is said that it is permissible to kill the Buddha, that is, to deny the source and origin

Figure 15. The Eternal Process of Change: Buddha's View.

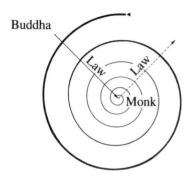

of life. It is also permissible to kill the Monk, to deny this teacher, that sect, those individual manifestations. But it is forbidden to kill the Law. That brings immediate retribution. The idea is the same.

45. Jesus said: "Grapes are not harvested from thorns, nor figs gathered from thistles, for they bear no fruit. A good man brings forth good from his [good] treasure. A bad man brings forth evil from the evil treasure, which is in his heart, and speaks evil things. For out of the abundance of the heart he brings forth ill."

This is another verse on cause and effect. Jesus is saying "by their fruits ye shall know them." [*Matthew* 7:20] The seed is father to the harvest. The harvest is child of the seed. Of course, good and evil are relative, not absolute. By evil Jesus means something more like imbalance. Thinking and acting always go together. Mind and body are one. If our treasure is good—an understanding of One Infinity and its Order—all of our actions will be harmonious and peaceful. Life established on this foundation will yield good fruit. If our treasure is evil—an ignorance of the eternal laws of change and seeking after ephemeral things—everything we do will lead to disorder. Life established on this foundation will be barren.

46. Jesus said: "From Adam until John the Baptist, among those born of women there is none higher than John the Baptist, so that his eyes will not be divided. But I have said that whoever among you becomes as a child shall know the Kingdom, and he shall be higher than John."

"Those born of women" is a traditional figure of speech for a human being. From the time Adam and Eve ate from the Tree of the Knowledge of Good and Evil until the time Jesus lived, the modern civilization of Greece and Rome, few knew how to return to Paradise. John the Baptist was a righteous man. He sought passionately for the Kingdom of Heaven. Though he did not know the laws of the infinite universe, John was farseeing, less blind and dualistic than the rest. But you who know the teachings of the Living Father and become like children—marveling at the world of One Infinity around you and keeping a beginner's mind—can see even more clearly. You are higher than John and will live in Paradise, knowing that we are always in the Kingdom of Heaven.

47. Jesus said: "It is impossible for a man to mount two horses and to draw two bows. And it is impossible for a servant to serve two masters, lest he honor the one and show disrespect to the other. No man drinks old wine and immediately desires to drink new wine. New wine is not put into old wineskins lest they burst, nor old wine into a new wineskin, lest it spoil it. An old patch is not sewn on a new garment, because it would tear."

What are the two horses, the two bows, the two masters, the two types of wine, and the two garments? To understand the choice before us, we have to look at the relation of *will* and *desire*.

In the long journey of life, we appear and then disappear. We come from and return to One Infinity. Our universe is now expanding logarithmically. Spirallic force is generated in every direction from expanding galaxies. Everywhere centripetal force

Figure 16. The Spiral of the Infinite Universe.

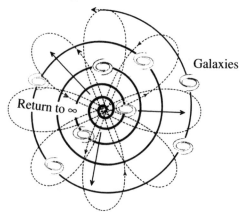

balances centrifugal force (*see* Figure 16). We receive force or energy from the center of the universe, from our own galaxy, from our solar system, and from the earth's center. At the end of this long spiral of materialization is human consciousness. After we come to this earth and manifest ourselves as human beings, we start to go back in the other direction. We spiritualize ourselves, developing our consciousness and judgment, eventually returning to One Infinity.

Will is the endless course of life, the Order of the Universe. We can't change it. Everything is going toward that. It is the big current. Who decides? Infinite you decides.

Within this big current of universal life, smaller waves are rising and falling. Some go up and down, some go zigzag. Some are big, others are small. *Desire* is that fluctuation. Our physical manifestation and spiritual manifestation are functions of will. Within that larger current, we are always swimming and traveling. But constant changes and fluctuations are a product of desire. Desire is the infinitesimally small you. When desire fluctuates, you sometime lose sight of will. Jesus wanted to talk about will, the big current of life, going from the beginningless beginning to the endless end. But people, his disciples included, wanted to talk about desire. He keeps telling them that will is more important than desire.

Conscience arises when desire becomes off track or extreme. You lose your will. Will—the Order of the Universe, the Holy Spirit—then tries to bring you back from your desire. The whole universe is always trying to balance and harmonize. If you are modest and humble in your way of life, especially in your way of eating, your desire is less and your will is strengthened. Small fluctuations are still there, but you feel them less and are less attached to them. Everyone has conscience. Conscience is the balancing power. Conscience tells us, "This is not good," or "I feel bad." Conscience is trying to turn your direction from desire to will. If you don't feel conscience, your eating is very bad and your intuition is very clouded. Then accidents or sicknesses arise to wake you up.

There are two types of conscience: 1) learned conscience—this is the moral standard you learn after you are born. A simple example is learning to walk on the left-hand side of the road. If you are hit by a car while you are walking on the right-hand side of the road, then you immediately know that you have done a wrong thing. 2) Native, genuine conscience—this is the universal conscience that everyone has regardless of any nation, any education, any time, any place. An obvious example of this is to honor your parents.

Physically, if you make some mistake, you will become sick. You will feel pain. No one can escape from this phenomenon. Throughout the world, throughout the ages, no one has escaped from the consequences of their actions. This pain has to be suffered. This is universal conscience. Many people think that physical sickness and mental suffering have nothing at all to do with conscience. They cannot understand where conscience comes from. Pain is nothing more than a manifestation in the body of universal conscience. When you become sick, it means that you have violated the Order of the Universe, and you must suffer. And when you violate the Order of the Universe, then you will also suffer mentally and spiritually. That also is a result of conscience.

In many instances, the universal and learned conscience stand in conflict with each other. There are many instances where a person who wishes to live according to his genuine, universal conscience is often considered by society to be an outlaw or heretic. In order for this person to live according to genuine, universal conscience he or she may have to violate the learned conscience which the society has erected around them. If these two are in conflict, then you cannot live according to both of them at the same time. You have to make a choice. This conflict is what Jesus was referring to when he said that a person cannot serve two masters at one time or pull two bows. You have to make a choice. You have to serve the master of learned conscience or the master of genuine, universal conscience.

When you choose the genuine, universal conscience as your master, the possibility exists that you will be persecuted by those who live according to the learned, socialized conscience. When you choose to live according to the learned, socialized conscience, the possibility exists that your natural quality will suffer as a result of the balancing effects of natural order. You may become sick, or unhappy, or frustrated. Either way, however, you must choose. You cannot have both.

When you return to living according to your natural, genuine conscience, ultimately you will become healthier, happier, and more peaceful. Life becomes so simple. But when you follow the artificial, learned conscience, then life becomes so difficult: you have to get degrees, you have to get a certificate, you have to get a license, you have to have an occupation, you have to have a Social Security number. Life becomes so complicated.

Jesus is warning us not to devote our main attention in life to trifles. These trifling things can occupy a small portion of our thoughts, but we should not let them control the direction our life is headed in. Money and material possessions and external organizations are passing matters. We can surrender ourself to them in a small way. But what we cannot surrender is our endless dream in life. And even if millions of people are opposed to us, still we should pursue it. We should always pursue our dream and make it greater and greater—infinite and eternal. That is our universal conscience. If we live by that, then we are living far beyond any generation or country. We are no longer limited to being a Christian or a Jew, a Buddhist or a Taoist, a citizen of the Roman Empire or the United States or even the world. We are a citizen of the entire universe. We are seeing the common thread that connects all people, all religions, all places, all times.

48. Jesus said: "If two make peace with each other in this one house, they shall say to the mountain: 'Move,' and it shall be moved."

The "one house" is the infinite universe. The "two" are complementary opposites such as man and woman, light and dark, centrifugality and centripetality. Making peace means knowing how to harmonize and balance yin and yang—the two forces that make up all phenomena. The mountain is a symbol of something immovable. But the immovable can be moved by understanding the natural flow of energy. If we look at the mountain like all phenomena as a wave of energy extending from the distant past into the distant future, we see that it will eventually become a plain and then a valley. It will someday turn into its opposite.

Jesus is saying that if we know how to apply yin and yang and harmonize them, we can achieve anything. We can transform sickness into health, poverty into wealth, sadness into joy. Through knowledge of universal order, all things are possible. His teaching is nothing but the unifying principle of macrobiotics—life according to the great view.

The mountain also stands for reaching the level of supreme and universal consciousness, seeing in all directions. At the level of universal consciousness in which we become one with God or One Infinity, whatever we want to do, we can do. Whatever we want to achieve, we can achieve. That is the kind of freedom Jesus was talking about. Any kind of dream we have can be realized. There are no limits. Infinity means that we can endlessly realize and enjoy our dream. Life becomes play. We create our own adventure. At the level of supreme consciousness, there is no particular set purpose to life. We set the purpose.

Whatever we would like to do, we can do. Whatever we would like to be, we can be. That is our dream, that is our purpose.

49. Jesus said: "Blessed are the solitary ones and the chosen, for you shall find the Kingdom. From it you came and to it you shall return."

Who are "the solitary ones"? The solitary ones are those who know Oneness—God or the Infinite Order of the Universe. They don't depend on anyone. They take care of themselves. They can stand alone. Who are "the chosen"? The chosen are those who chose themselves. Who chose you to come to this world? You chose yourself. In the world of the infinite universe, in the Kingdom of Heaven, there is no voting system. You must choose yourself. You alone are responsible for your destiny. You alone choose how you will live your life. You decide: "I will go this way. I will seek that way." Your health, happiness, and freedom depend entirely upon you.

Those who themselves choose to seek truth continuously, to live the Order of the Universe, are the blessed. They come from the Kingdom of Heaven, this wonderful infinite universe, and remember their origin. From there, they physicalized upon this earth. Then again, after their life here, they will return to the infinite universe. Those who seek shall find these things. Therefore they are blessed. Origin and destiny are one. Unless you elect yourself, you are just experiencing the vicissitudes of life. Without knowing your origin or future, you become more and more attached to the ephemeral world. Your sickness, unhappiness, and difficulties mount and you never discover, nor enter, the Kingdom.

50. Jesus said: "If they say to you: 'Where have you come from?', say to them: 'We have come from the Light, where the Light came into being by itself. It [shone forth] and revealed itself in their image.' If they say to you: 'Who are you?', say: 'We are his children and we are the chosen of the

Living Father.' If they ask you: 'What is the sign of your
Father in you?', say to them: 'It is movement and rest.'"

Jesus is talking to his disciples about spreading the teachings of
eternal truth. Because the disciples go from village to village,
they would be questioned about the place of their origin. Instead
of saying they are from such-and-such a town or village, Jesus
tells them to say they come from the light. The place where the
light originated through itself is the seventh heaven—God or
One Infinity. The place where it shone forth and revealed itself
in their image is the first heaven—this world, earth. Jesus is
teaching them to say that they came from the infinite universe,
physicalized themselves, and will go back to infinity. He is telling the disciples to say they come from One Infinity, not Jerusalem, Rome, or New York.

On the Spiral of Life, light includes waves, vibrations, energy
(*see* Figure 17). This part of the spiral is not visible. Yin and
yang are also not visible. But waves and vibrations are the first

Figure 17. The World of Vibration.

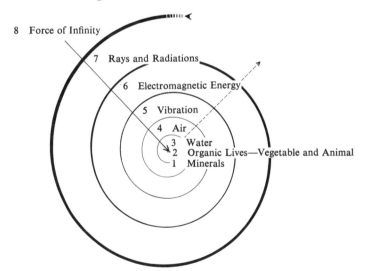

stage of manifestation. We have materialized ourselves from that ocean of vibration. Light is only one small phenomenon of this world of vibrations. Jesus chose this particular aspect of the spiral to talk about because most people cannot understand beyond that. Any further—yin and yang and One Infinity—people's understanding is very conceptual. But ordinary people can see and feel the world of vibration, light. From there, other worlds, including our world, were born. "It [shone forth] and revealed itself in their image." Many images, or forms, came out from the light.

If they say to you "Who are you?" say "We are his children and we are the chosen of the Living Father." What is "his"? What is "chosen"? And what is the "Living Father"? Again Jesus is talking about the seventh heaven. The Living Father is One Infinity. We are all sons and daughters of that endlessly moving, changing process of universal life. We have all chosen to come here of our own accord. If you understand your true origin and destiny, even though many people do not understand you, you are blessed because you will discover the Kingdom—the entire universe and its marvelous order.

One time the people stoned Jesus. They asked him how old he was, and he said he was older than Abraham. People didn't understand and got very angry. On this occasion he also meant he had come from infinity. Life is eternal. Many people couldn't understand what he was saying. But they were thinking in a limited way and couldn't understand him.

"If they ask you: 'What is the sign of your Father in you?', say to them: 'It is movement and rest.' " In our terms, movement and rest are yang and yin, action and inaction, centripetality and centrifugality, time and space, front and back, inside and outside. That is the sign of the Living Father—the everchanging, moving infinite universe. Everyone and everything are characterized by these forces, tendencies, or qualities.

Jesus is teaching his disciples the unifying principle of yin and yang. This principle was known throughout the ancient world. In the *Book of Genesis*, God is known by two names:

Elohim and Adonai. Elohim is justice and Adonai is mercy.
Elohim is strength, action, righteousness. Adonai is gentleness,
inaction, compassion. Together they make up the two hands of
God. The traditional phase "The Lord our God is one" [*Deuteronomy* 6:4] is recited in Hebrew as "Elohim and Adonai are
one." In other words, yang and yin are one. "Look upon all the
works of the most high," *Ecclesiasticus* 33:15 states: "They,
likewise, are in pairs, one the opposite of the other." But by
Jesus's time, this dynamic understanding of reality had been
lost. He is calling them back to this way of seeing the world. It is
the essence of his teaching.

**51. His disciples said to him: "When will the final rest of the
dead take place and when will the new world come?" He
said to them: "What you are waiting for has already come,
but you do not know it."**

The disciples are asking Jesus when the happiest time would
come. He tells them that Paradise is already here, if they understand the Order of the Universe. The New Age is here and has
been here all the time. Yet you expect it at some future time.
There is no special time in the future when it will come. When
you understand, you can see that it is here already. But since you
don't understand, you cannot see. That is what Jesus was saying.
The endless Order of the Universe is always here in this world.
Wonderful life is here. But you don't know that.

**52. His disciples said to him: "Twenty-four prophets have
spoken in Israel and they all spoke of you." He said to them:
"You have denied the Living One who is in your presence
and you speak of the dead."**

The disciples are constantly quoting the scriptures. The twenty-
four prophets may refer to the twenty-four books in the Hebrew
Bible. The Messiah of popular expectation was imagined to be a
military conqueror like David or a high priest like Elijah who

would deliver the Jewish people from foreign bondage. The disciples are continually wondering whether Jesus is the Messiah.

Jesus replies that they have ignored the infinite living universe—the true bringer of freedom that is before their eyes, constantly creating life. Instead they are speaking about dead concepts and doctrines that are not living at all. Jesus is strongly telling them to turn their seeking of a messiah and savior to the understanding of the Infinite One and its order. He is exhorting them to behold the world around them and discover the Order of the Universe. Wonderful things are going on day by day, moment to moment, from the endlessly long past to the endlessly long future. Why do you need to wait until someone comes to save you?

53. His disciples said to him: "Is circumcision profitable?" He said to them: "If it were profitable, their father would beget them circumcised from their mother. But the true circumcision in spirit is profitable in all respects."

First, about physical circumcision, Jesus is saying that if it were natural, baby boys would already be born without a foreskin. Since they were born with a foreskin, they should respect the Order of the Universe and accept the way they were naturally born. That is the best way. The same thing is true today in respect to tonsils. Millions of people face having their tonsils taken out. But if tonsils are not needed, why were we born with them? The tonsils are an important part of the lymphatic system and produce antibodies that help neutralize excessive food and drink. However, if we eat excessively foods high in simple sugar and foods rich in fat, as well as other unhealthy items, the tonsils become overactived and chronically swollen. Cutting them out weakens our natural immune system even more. Yet because of simple ignorance, the medical profession continues to take out people's tonsils.

What is the origin of circumcision? According to the *Book of*

Genesis, Abraham started this custom to mark off his descendants. But if the real purpose was identification, why not just tattoo them? No, Abraham needed men who matured quickly. Hormone secretion becomes active by stimulation. By exposing the very sensitive end part of the penis, the hormone system becomes active. As a result, quick maturity develops—mentally and physically. Abraham was a very smart person. The Jewish people at that time were in a minority. There were many tribes competing and surrounding them. In order to make the Jewish people mature quickly, he recommended this method. As a result, they became very good warriors, very capable administrators, very smart leaders. The Bible is full of the exploits of precocious young boys like Joseph, David, Daniel, and young Jesus himself.

Jesus says, however, that such physical circumcision is unnecessary and unnatural. Actually, it is more yangizing than natural maturity, leading to a tendency toward competitiveness and cleverness. Rather we should circumcise our spirit. By this he means wiping away delusions, forgetting about dead concepts and doctrines. Making up your mind, "I will grow with the Order of the Universe. I will realize and enter the Kingdom of Heaven." That is true circumcision in spirit. That is helpful in every way.

54. Jesus said: "Blessed are the poor, for yours is the Kingdom of Heaven."

This is one of the ten beatitudes from the Sermon on the Mount. Most of the ten are found in the *Gospel of Thomas*, though they are not grouped together as in the other gospels. They may originally have been part of a commentary by Jesus on the Ten Commandments.

Like other aspects of his teachings, the beatitudes are based on the principles of yin and yang. Times of suffering are balanced with times of happiness. Times of hunger will be balanced with times of plenty. Jesus did not attempt to do away with or destroy the times of difficulty. Rather, he taught how to affirm these times of difficulty in order to work through to the times of happiness and fulfillment. He taught that in times of difficulty, poverty, and suffering, we should not try to get rid of those things but accept them and try to understand their true origin and development.

At the level of supreme consciousness—becoming a person of light—you will no longer wish to destroy either joy or sadness, day or night, life or death. At that level you embrace all these things just as they are. And you can understand that when you have happiness, you will also have unhappiness. When you have unhappiness, you know that happiness is also coming. When you are happy, you are not arrogant about it. Rather you feel sad because although you know that you are happy, you know that other people are unhappy. When you are unhappy, you don't feel particularly unhappy or sad. Rather you are grateful because you know that from this experience you can learn new things, and you know that happiness will soon be coming to you, and you realize that through this experience you can help many other people. Those who are grateful for their poverty, sickness, and difficulties are truly blessed.

55. Jesus said: "He who does not hate his father and his mother will not be able to be a disciple of Me. And [he who does not] hate his brothers and his sisters and bear his cross in My way will not be worthy of Me."

The fifth of the Ten Commandments is to honor your mother and father. Jesus appears to be asking his disciples to do just the opposite: to hate their parents and other family members. But here he is not referring to physical parents and brothers and sisters so much as cultural, social, or religious parents and family. By mother and father, he means whatever it is that we honor foremost. It could be our physical parents, our religion, modern science and medicine, wealth and success, or other concepts, beliefs, and attainments. Jesus is saying that all the artificial, conceptual, and delusional systems from which we seek happiness must be abandoned if we are to become a true follower of One Infinity (Me). To hate your mother and father means to break those attachments.

The second part, Jesus's injunction to bear the cross, is also found in the *Gospels of Matthew*, *Mark*, and *Luke*. Bearing the cross does not refer so much to undergoing suffering, though as we saw in the previous verse that is an excellent teacher and way to learn the Order of the Universe. The cross is "a sign of the Father" (*see Verse* 50), a symbol of yin and yang. It combines vertical yin energy and horizontal yang energy. It has front and back, up and down, left and right, ascending and descending sides. Bearing the cross in "My way"—in an infinite way—is to learn how to unify and balance opposites. Jesus is saying, "Take up yin and yang—the Order of the Infinite Universe—and follow me."

56. Jesus said: "He who has known the world has found a corpse, and he who has found a corpse, of him the world is not worthy."

Whoever has studied dualistic systems, beliefs, and ways of life has found only dead knowledge but not Life itself—the world of eternal health, happiness, and peace. However, he who has discovered how truly lifeless are religion, politics, science, education, and other modern institutions, that world is no longer satisfying. The infinite life alone is worthy of his or her faith.

57. Jesus said: "The Kingdom of the Father is like a man who possessed [good] seed. His enemy came by night and sowed weeds among the good seed. The man did not allow [the servants] to pull up the weeds. He said to them: 'I fear that you will go to pull up the weeds and uproot the grain along with them.' For on the day of the harvest, the weeds will be clearly visible, and they will be uprooted and burned."

98

Life is a mixture of many things. To our human mind, food
crops are good, while weeds are bad. However, to the eye of
God, good and evil, faith and doubt, and other pairs of opposites
are complementary. In addition to nourishing other forms of life,
weeds strengthen the crops growing in the field. They break up
the ground, collect moisture, and keep away insects and birds.
After the grain ripens and is collected, then the wheat can be cut
with a sickle and the weeds can be left to fall so that they are not
gathered into the sheaves. Later, the weeds can be pulled up,
dried, and be burned for fuel or be used as a natural fertilizer for
the next crop.

In this verse, Jesus is once again teaching eternal truths about
the dynamic interrelation of all things. The wise farmer, like the
Kingdom of Heaven, embraces everything and uses principles of
yin and yang to separate things and make order. But he understands the universal process of spirallic growth and lets things
ripen in their own time. He doesn't rush in and make everything
conform to his small i—his ephemeral, delusional self—but
harmonizes himself with the marvelous Order of the Infinite
Universe around him.

Failure to observe this principle has resulted in modern agriculture and the development of artificial fertilizers, pesticides,
monocropping, hybridized seeds, and other dualistic approaches
to farming. The result has been rapid decline of our human species through artificial and highly processed foods. If modern day
farmers could understand just this one parable of Jesus, they
could begin to reverse the current epidemic of cancer, heart disease, mental illness, infertility, AIDS, and other degenerative
and immune-deficiency disorders. Through natural agricultural
practices that respected weeds, insects, birds, and mammals as
part of a larger whole and that produced healthy organic foods,
they could help transform the modern world from a hell into a
paradise.

**58. Jesus said: "Blessed is the man who has suffered, for he
has found Life."**

Suffering is the gateway to wisdom. Many people do not understand this. Today, for instance, when they find they have cancer,
many people get very depressed or angry. They feel that they
have done nothing to deserve it. They go to church or temple
every week and give money to their favorite charities. They get
very upset and think God is punishing them. Or they think there
is no God and life is meaningless. They go to the hospital, have
the tumor cut out or burned away, and carry on their life as before, praying that their cancer has gone away for good. But later
it comes back somewhere else in a more serious form. They get
upset again, have another operation, use up all their hard earned
money, and eventually die in great pain and sorrow.

This is another instance of *Saying* 41: "[H]e who does not
have [an understanding of the Order of the Universe], from him
even the little which he has shall be taken." Instead of this blind
approach, we should self-reflect. What is the true cause of my
cancer? Does it come about because of something I might have
done? Is my way of life, including way of thinking, eating, and
relating to other people, imbalanced? If I change and try to harmonize with the marvelous world of infinite beauty and order
around me, can't I reverse this condition? Such people who seek
to understand the Order of the Universe discover that nothing is
impossible for someone who understands the unifying principle
of yin and yang. Through proper eating and balance of activities,
their tumor naturally shrinks and disappears. They discover a
wonderful secret: the greatest unhappiness is the source of their
greatest happiness. As many friends have declared after changing their lifestyle and eating macrobiotically, "Cancer was the
greatest thing that ever happened to me. I learned that I had created it myself through years of wrong eating and wrong way of
life. And what I made, I can unmake. After becoming macrobiotic, learning to cook and eat properly, and changing my view of
life and way of living, I never felt better. My life is immeasura-
bly enriched." Thousands of such personal accounts are there.

This is Jesus's teaching. Accept responsibility for your own
poverty, sickness, and suffering. If you try to escape from it, you

will only make yourself more miserable and never have a chance to become happy. Everyone must experience the hardships and sufferings they have created. This is the Order of the Universe. This is the principle of life.

After several generations of disciples, Jesus's teachings were transformed from one in which hardships were faced into one in which the leaders claimed that people's misery could be relieved by believing in the Church or in Christ as the savior. Salvation in terms of getting out of difficulties became a prime calling card of these new forms of religion. But this "salvation" goes against the Order of the Universe which holds that if joy is there, sadness will also be there; if day is there, night is there; if life is there, death is there; if happiness is there, unhappiness is there. These opposites are always found together, limiting, defining, and complementing each other. Without one, the other would not exist.

59. Jesus said: "Behold the Living One while you are alive, lest you die and seek to see him and be unable to see."

Jesus warns his disciples never to lose sight of One Infinity (the Living One), their origin and destiny. If they don't seek out and find the principles of eternal life—the spiral, yin and yang, the Five Trees of Paradise—in this life, they will surely not find God's kingdom in the world to come because it too is governed by the same order. In fact, so long as they remain blind to the Order of the Universe, they will have to return again and again to be reborn upon the earth until they learn to properly nourish their minds and bodies and refine their spirits.

60. [They saw] a Samaritan carrying a lamb on his way to Judea. He said to his disciples: "[Why] is this man [carrying] a lamb with him?" They said to him: "So that he may slay it and eat it." He said to them: "As long as it is alive, he will not eat it, but only if he has slain it and it becomes a corpse." They said: "Otherwise he will be unable to do it." He said to

them: "You, too, seek a place for yourselves in rest, lest you become corpses and be eaten."

The Samaritans were a neighboring people who worshiped the Jewish God and journeyed to the Temple in Jerusalem to commemorate the Passover and other festivals. Jesus asks his disciples why the Samaritan was traveling to Jerusalem with a lamb. The disciples replied that he was going to have it ritually slain for the Passover meal. Jesus uses this custom to comment about life and death in the modern world.

In this passage, he is teaching that if we live in delusion, we will be killed and eaten like the sacrificial lamb. Our reality and being will be destroyed, used up, and devoured as a consequence of our own illusory beliefs. But if we find One Infinity and live in it, we will neither be slain nor consumed by our ephemeral attachments.

61. Jesus said: "Two will rest on a sofa. One will die, and one will live." Salome said: "Who are you, man, [and by what authority do] you recline upon my seat and eat from my table?" Jesus said to her: "I am he who is from the Whole, to me was given of the things of my Father." Salome said: "I am your disciple." [Jesus said to her:] "Therefore I say, if he is whole, he will be filled with light, but if he is divided, he will be filled with darkness."

The first part of this verse is paralleled in the New Testament. In *Luke* 17:34-36, Jesus says: "I tell you, in that night there shall be two men in one bed; the one shall be taken, and the other shall be left. Two women shall be grinding together; the one shall be taken, and the other left. Two men shall be in the field; the one shall be taken, and the other left."

Why do some people discover the Order of the Universe and others never find it? Why do some people find the light and others remain in darkness? To answer this question, we must look at this problem from a wider view. We must see constitution and condition. We must see not only the physical constitution but also the spiritual constitution. We must see not only the physical condition but also the mental and psychological condition.

Where is the constitution—our inherited qualities and characteristics—mainly formed? In the mother's womb together with our ancestors' biological and spiritual inheritances. During the embryonic period, the fetus increases in size three billion times. Then after we are born, our size increases only twenty to thirty times. How we develop in the womb has a big influence on our life. Besides food, we were strongly influenced by our mother's thinking, her emotions, and her way of life. Of course, the father's influence is also there by the quality of his sperm, his thinking, and his vibrations. The vibrational quality of our parents, and in particular our mother's way of eating and thinking during pregnancy, has a big influence on our constitution.

In addition, the constitution of our ancestors also influences us. For example, among our ancestors, if they were very spiritual, humble, hard-working people, our constitution will reflect these influences.

Beyond this, our constitution is affected by celestial influences and also by the earth's motion. We are influenced not only by the stars, the moon and the planets, and the energy coming in from billions of distant galaxies, but also by the climate, weather, and season. All these natural influences contribute to our constitution. We must see them.

Our constitution starts to grow as a result of these influences. But day by day, month by month, year by year, our condition is changing. Again, our condition is affected by present day astronomical influences like the stars' motion, planetary motion, and galactic motion, and also by the climate, season, temperature, and atmospheric energy. We may say this is heaven's condition.

But also we are constantly changing according to earth's condition. We change according to the changing quality of the soil, water, and air that we take in every day. For instance, the air may be heavily polluted if we live in the city or it may be fresh if we go to the mountains. The water we drink may be chlorinated or treated by various other chemicals. Or it may be very pure well water or mountain stream water. The soil may be very acidic or very dry. These conditions on earth influence our daily condition.

Then between the influence of heaven and earth, we are greatly influenced by the quality and quantity of our daily food and drink. And this too, of course, is affected by the season and climate, as well as the condition of the soil, air, and water. Our food represents a combination of heaven and earth's influences. Other influences from the outside also have an effect upon us. Day to day we are affected by other people, the media, books, schools, and social factors. They are acting upon our condition and have a basic influence on the way we look at life.

Our dream in life is shaped by both our constitution and condition. The tendency of our dream is passed on from our ancestors, but the clarity of this dream and the way we pursue it depend upon our condition and our present influences.

For example, fear governs many people's lives. Where does fear begin? Constitution or condition? Most fear begins here, from our ancestral influence. Of course, after you are born, the type of family, the type of education, and the type of society you live in influence this. If every Sunday, for instance, you go to church and are told that you are a sinner, that hell is waiting for you, and that even from the time of birth you are guilty, you can easily create such an image in your consciousness and fear will grow.

Many people develop such fear and live their whole lives in darkness. And yet, under the same influences, other people react and think differently. They might say, "Yes, maybe I am a sinner now, but I will begin to live correctly and by that I will change my destiny in a more positive way. I will find the light." The difference in the way individuals react is due to ancestral heritage. Although two people receive the same teachings, one person will take a more negative approach and develop fear, while another person will take a more positive approach and begin to change himself. This is what Jesus meant by saying one person will live and one will die.

In the second part of the verse, Jesus is asked once again who he is and where he comes from. He tells Salome that he is a son of the infinite universe (the Whole) and acting as its representative. She is astonished and asks to become his student. He replies that the things of the Living Father are freely available to everyone. If she is filled with light (understands the Order of the Universe), she can become the same as him. She can act as representative of One Infinity and live in the Kingdom of Heaven. But if her mind is dualistic (divided), she will be filled with darkness and not live in the Kingdom.

62. Jesus said: "I reveal My mysteries to those [deserving of My] mysteries. Do not let your left hand know what your right hand is doing."

By mysteries, Jesus does not mean secret teachings. Often times there will be a secret form of the religion involving initiation rites, oral transmission, and other so-called secret teachings. Gnosticism has this, as do certain forms of Buddhism and Islam, closed fraternal societies, and some Christian sects. Only a select few members of the religion are allowed to participate in the secret forms of religious practice.

These secrets are meaningless for the real happiness of life. They exist only to maintain authority. These religions have many interesting teachings and practices, but in comparison with an understanding of the Order of the Universe, they are small and fragmentary. The newborn baby already enjoys a happy life without learning any special teaching. The people who maintain religions with secret teachings are generally eating excessively spicy foods, dairy products, or honey and other simple sugars, as well as foods rich in hard fat, all of which tend to contribute to a secretive mentality that wants to mystify as well as be mystified.

The teachings of eternal truth are available to everyone. There are no miracles, no secrets. As soon as you discover something, you must spread it. You must give it away. You must share your knowledge and understanding. You must help reduce people's suffering and lead them to the light. That is the best way. That is Jesus's way.

However, there are some portions which cannot be explained yet. First, because they take time, and secondly, because people's health and consciousness must be stabilized. Until you experience and understand basic life, such as proper cooking, natural agriculture, healthy exercise, sound mind, and harmonious daily human relations, it will be difficult for you to develop the deeper understanding of life. These things are not secret, but they are difficult for you to know if you do not understand the preliminary principles. That is why you must wait and practice. But day by day, year by year, they will be released as your health and consciousness improve. In that sense, the mysterious or untaught teachings are there. But they should not be understood as being held back. You can understand them by yourself, through your own experience, if you really try. You don't need a special teacher.

The second part of this verse, dealing with right and left hands, has many echoes in the Bible. For example, God asks Jonah: "And should not I spare Nineveh, that great city, wherein are more than sixscore thousand persons that cannot discern between their right hand and their left hand . . . ?" [*Jonah* 4:11].

Through the centuries, many readers of the Bible and commentators have identified the right hand with good (might, strength, and life) and the left hand with evil (weakness, deception, death). They assume that God means to destroy Nineveh because the people can't distinguish between good and evil. But this is not their meaning. Right and left are complementary opposites—yin and yang. Everything in the relative world is moving and changing. Everything is made up of front and back, inside and outside, above and below, center and periphery, left and right, and numerous other relations. There is no absolute good or evil. The reason Nineveh is bent on destruction is because its inhabitants have forgotten the Order of the Universe and yin and yang. They are bringing sickness, accident, war, or other calamity upon themselves.

In this passage about left and right hands in the *Gospel of Thomas*, which is also found in the *Gospel of Matthew*, Jesus is teaching his disciples to see from a unifying rather than a dualistic perspective. Compared to the whole—One infinity and its endless order—yin and yang, up and down, left and right are relative. The disciples, for example, are viewing life from the contemporary Jewish standpoint. They don't see it from the Roman perspective, and vice versa. The same thing is true today. Many Americans are convinced their way of life is superior and the Soviets are evil, while the Communists believe socialism is the fulfillment of humanity and capitalism is immoral. There are many other polarities in the modern world: Arabs vs. Jews, Catholics vs. Protestants, Protestant sects vs. Protestant sects, and so on.

In order to realize health, happiness, and peace, we must take into account the interests and welfare of all concerned and view life from the largest possible view—*macro bios*. We need to learn how to discern between right and left, as well as balance, harmonize, and synthesize them when necessary. There is no sense of good and evil. Jesus uses right and left like Lao Tzu in the *Tao Te Ching:* "The great Tao flows everywhere, both to the left and to the right."

"Do not let your left hand know what your right hand is doing" means act as a representative of One Infinity—the eternal you—not from your small self. See things from the view of universal consciousness. If you let your small self—either the right hand or the left hand—judge, evaluate, and decide your course of action, you will stumble and fall. You will never find lasting happiness. But if you act from your infinite self—encompassing both left and right—you will go with the Order of the Universe and endlessly realize your endless dream.

63. Jesus said: "There was a rich man who had much wealth.

He said: 'I will invest my money that I may sow and reap
and plant and fill my warehouses with the harvest, so that I
need nothing.' He resolved this in his heart, and that night
he died. Whoever has ears let him hear."

The rich and mighty shall become poor. The poor and meek
shall inherit the earth. The first shall become last, the last shall
become first. There are many such sayings attributed to Jesus.
Once again, he is talking about the universal laws of harmony
and change (*see* the Appendix). Unless we continually distribute
everything that we receive, we will become full. Once we become full, we start to turn into our opposite. We start to decline
and become empty. Such is the law of life. If we think only of
ourselves, we shall never be satisfied, and the little that we have
will be taken from us. True happiness consists in endless giving.
In matters of food, for example, we should eat to only about 80
percent of our stomach's capacity. If we do that, we are always
sound, energetic, and have a good appetite for whatever we want
to do. So long as we are a little empty, we can receive more. But
if we eat to the full extent of capacity or overeat, then our energy
and appetite naturally wane. The same thing with money,
wealth, goods, honors, titles, knowledge. If we don't share our
happiness and good fortune with others, we shall lose everything.

**64. Jesus said: "A man had guests, and after preparing din-
ner, he sent his servant to invite the guests. He went to the
first and said to him: 'My master summons you.' The man
said: 'I have a transaction to settle with some merchants.
They are coming to see me in the evening. I must go and
present them my claim. I ask to be excused from the dinner.'
He went to another and said to him: 'My master has sum-
moned you.' He said to him: 'I have bought a house and
have been called away for the day. I have no time.' He came
to another and said to him: 'My master summons you.' He
said to him: 'My friend is to be married and I must arrange**

the banquet. I regret that I shall not be able to come and pray to be excused.' He went to another and said to him: 'My master summons you.' He said to him: 'I bought a farm and have to collect the rent. I am unable to attend. Please excuse me.' The servant returned to his master: 'Those whom you invited to dinner have excused themselves.' The master said to his servant: 'Go out to the streets, bring back whomever you find, so that they may partake of the meal [with Me]. Tradesmen and merchants shall not enter the abode of my Father.' "

The theme of this verse is similar to the last one. The man or Father giving the banquet is One Infinity. Everyone is invited to dine on the marvelous Order of the Universe, but most people are too busy with various human affairs and trifling things. One person has business to transact. Another has a real estate appointment. A third has to cater a wedding. A fourth has to collect rent from a tenant. Just like these people, we come up with endless excuses for not seeking eternal truth.

"I'm sorry, but it's my bowling night."
"I'd love to, but I'm expecting the plumber."
"I would but I don't have the ZIP code."

We are too busy to eat well, study yin and yang, and change ourselves in harmony with the wonderful world of infinity around us. We are too preoccupied with affairs and things of small value, neglecting to seek the true understanding of life and helping other people and making a better world.

So long as we are following the small i we can never live in the Kingdom of Heaven. Those who will find it are those who are not attached to property or riches. The people out on the roads who Jesus mentions are the passers-by in *Verse* 42. The poor, the sick, and the persecuted are not blinded by possessions and petty concerns. They don't know where their next meal will come from. They don't know where they will sleep. They don't know whether they can survive the cold weather. Their minds are open. Their hearts are very grateful. They are content with very little. They are seeking a true end to their suffering and realization of enduring health, happiness, and peace. They will find the way to God and feast on his Endless Order.

65. He said: "A good man had a vineyard. He leased it to some tenants so that they would work it and he would receive the produce from them. He sent his servant to collect the fruit from the tenants. They laid hold of his servant and beat him. A little more and they would have killed him. The servant came back and reported to his master. His master said: 'Perhaps he did not know them.' He sent another servant, and the tenants beat him also. Then the owner sent his son. He said: 'Perhaps they will respect my son.' Knowing that he was the heir to the vineyard, the tenants seized him and killed him. Whoever has ears let him hear."

This is known as the Parable of the Wicked Husbandmen. It is also found in the *Gospels of Mark, Matthew*, and *Luke*. In the usual interpretation, the vineyard is Israel. The tenants are the Scribes, Pharisees, and other rulers and leaders. The servants are the prophets. The son is Christ. The final punishment (explicit in the New Testament versions, implied here) is the ruin of Israel. This interpretation is too limiting. In the largest, most universal sense, the vineyard is the infinite universe, our Big Self. We have all come to this earthly paradise to live together in health, happiness, and peace. These are the fruits to be enjoyed. The servants that have come to help us enjoy these fruits include all manifested things, such as animals, vegetables, and stones, but also sickness, suffering, and difficulties. Everything can teach us about the endless Order of the Universe. Everything changes according to yin and yang.

The basic principle of life, as we saw in the last several verses, is endless giving. By giving back to nature, nature constantly gives to us. But if we mistreat these servants and enjoy

110

the fruits only for ourselves, we are violating that Order. But the infinite universe is very patient. Perhaps we didn't understand. It tries again to alert us. We get many second chances.

For example, if we eat excessively, we get a cold. Sneezing, coughing, and fever are wonderful adjustment mechanisms alerting us to an imbalance in our way of life. They are servants of universal order and should be treated with respect. They must not be "beaten" down with aspirin and pills but allowed to take their course or be balanced naturally through safe, simple health preparations or home remedies. But if we artificially suppress these symptoms and continue our improper and disorderly way of life, the universe will send us more serious symptoms. The next time we go to the doctor, we may find that we have a cyst or stones. This is a sign of chronic disorder in our way of life. If we again don't pay heed to our way of eating and thinking and merely have the cyst or stone cut out, the next time we may find that we have cancer. Now it is a question of life or death. But the infinite universe—our Big I—gives us one last chance. He sends his son or daughter—that is anyone with understanding of the unifying principle—to show us a healthy alternative to surgery, radiation, or chemotherapy. If we reject that person or teachings of eternal truth, we shall perish away. Cancer is just one of endless examples. It could be family decline, the spread of crime in the community, or war.

66. Jesus said: "Show me the stone that the builders have rejected; it is the cornerstone."

This saying is an allusion to two passages in the Old Testament. The first is *Psalm* 118:22: "The stone which the builders refused is become the head stone of the corner." The second comes in *Isaiah* 28:16: "Therefore thus saith the Lord God, Behold, I lay in Zion for a foundation a stone, a tried stone, a precious corner stone, a sure foundation: he that believeth shall not make haste."

The stone stands for different things. First, it represents people who don't fit into modern society and its conceptual and artificial systems. These persons include free-minded people who are seeking natural universal law and way of life. They may also include the poor, the oppressed, the sick, and those rejected by society. People like this shall find the Order of the Universe and be blessed.

Second, the stone represents faith. It is like the mountain in *Sayings* 48 and 106 that can be moved by "making the two one," that is by the application of yin and yang. The foundation of Jesus's teachings is faith in the Order of the Universe. It is not blind acceptance or belief.

Jesus is saying on this rock, on the unifying principle, erect your future. Build your temple of eternal life on a firm setting. Don't be hasty. Take your time, be patient, go step by step, grow logarithmically stone by stone.

67. Jesus said: "Whoever knows the Whole but fails to know himself lacks everything."

There are people who seek God only in words, beliefs, concepts, or other abstractions. They don't seek God in themselves, in their minds and bodies, in their food, in their daily life. They see God only in the sky, in DNA, or the periodic table. These are the people Jesus is talking about.

People who know themselves know how to self-reflect and how to change. Self-reflection and self-change are the solution for all sicknesses, all troubles, all family problems, all wars. If you change yourself, you do not need to worry about changing the environment, changing the government, or fighting things on the outside. The answer is so simple, and you can do it by your own will, through your own understanding. Use your understanding of One Infinity (the Whole) and its endless Order to make yourself into whatever you want. This is the freedom Jesus is teaching.

To enjoy this freedom, we need an understanding of yin and yang and a knowledge of how to practically apply it to our daily lives. Then with yin and yang, we select and prepare food and drink, exercise, pray, meditate, chant, use vibrations, and so on to change ourselves. We take in many things each day, like radiations and vibrations from deep space, air, sunlight, and the vibrations from our surroundings. But of all of the things we take in, we have the most control over food and drink. So this is what we change first. Through these we immediately stabilize our health and judgment. Then automatically the type of vibrations we attract, the amount of oxygen we use, the situations we encounter, and so on, will change. Those around us will see the tremendous change in us. They see that we are happier, healthier, more peaceful. As our condition changes, it will naturally influence them, and they will begin to change. From this tiny seed, one peaceful world can grow.

68. Jesus said: "Blessed are you when you are hated and persecuted, for you will find a place where you will not be pursued."

Hatred and persecution come in many guises. The obvious threats include criminals, terrorists, religious and racial fanatics, government agencies, and large standing armies. But actually, everyone is being threatened every day with murder. Everyone is being put on trial constantly. Everyone is testing your judgment.

Your parents test you with their sentimental love—too much care that will shield you from all suffering and difficulties. Other people driving cars are testing you, as they may run into you and take away your life. The boss of your company is testing you, determining whether or not you will trade away your whole precious life for money, medical coverage, and other fringe benefits. War is testing you, religion is testing you, school education is testing you. You are all being tested every day, and your judgment is being hammered by these tests. As a result, the weak ones are killed. They have an accident or get sick and end up committing suicide. Even after death, the funeral profession tests you, finding out how much money you have left and how much you can spend on the way to the cemetery.

If your judgment is immature, you will become a slave only to material wealth. If your consciousness becomes higher, you can be free from those threats, persecutors, or tests. You are surrounded by many educators who are hammering you. You must appreciate all those difficulties suffered. For instance, many food stores are carrying a great quantity of artificial foods. If we eat those things every day, then naturally we become weak.

Many authorities now agree that chemicalization contaminates water. The air is already contaminated by industries. You've been put in very heavily sick surroundings, but those surroundings are testing you. They are like angels who come down from the heavens to make your judgment higher and higher. They enable you to see where real freedom is. So let us appreciate those artificial foods that are prevailing in the modern world; let us appreciate the industries that produce them. Let us appreciate the institutions that perpetuate the way of life that supports them, because they are the great teachers of humanity. If we truly appreciate everything, we enter the Kingdom of Heaven and find that place where there is no persecution, only endless unfolding order and truth.

69. Jesus said: "Blessed are those who have been persecuted in their hearts, for they have truly known the Father. Blessed are the hungry, for the appetite of him who desires shall be satisfied."

The greatest persecution is not from outside. It is from inside. It is the basic sense of sin, guilt, and worthlessness in our hearts. When Moses and Jesus started to teach the unifying principle, there was no concept of original sin or guilt. It was only later when the disciples did not understand the true meaning of Moses and Jesus's words that the concepts of original sin and guilt were formed.

These later teachers were afraid of such things as unhappiness, misery, and poverty. They took refuge in the idea of a heaven and hell where the righteous would he rewarded and the unrighteous would be punished. They created these myths to cope with their lack of real understanding of the Order of the Universe or what Jesus refers to, in *Matthew* 6:33, as the Justice of the Kingdom of Heaven. They could not see that happiness and unhappiness follow each other, so they taught about the existence of hell, purgatory, and heaven as progressive stages of punishment and reward. Many people came to feel that if they made a mistake, then they must quickly correct themselves by going to confession. This concept was carried to the extreme where it was considered proper restitution to pay money in order to gain forgiveness from sin. This was the practice of indulgence selling which Martin Luther so strongly opposed.

The concept of sin and guilt is very firmly rooted in the Judeo-Christian tradition. It is laid forth with great emphasis in the story of the Garden of Eden. This is the event of the Original Sin. This is the story of Paradise Lost. In addition, this story is succeeded by the story of the murder of Abel by Cain. Tradition has it that after losing the Garden of Eden because of his pride, man turned to murdering his brother.

This symbolizes the social unrest that has plagued humanity ever since. After Jesus was crucified, the theory arose that he died to purify us from our sins and wipe away our guilt. That is where the idea of salvation came from.

In the Far East, the word for guilt is *tsumi*. Its literal meaning is "accumulation." Originally, there were two interpretations of *tsumi*. There was the heavenly accumulation and the earthly accumulation. The heavenly accumulation came from the sin of illusion—wrong or cloudy thinking. The earthly accumulation came from the sin of attachment to material things—for instance, when you destroy your neighbor's house. In other words, traditionally guilt was understood as an accumulation of excess yin or an accumulation of excess yang in thought and action.

Jesus's teaching is like this. There is no original sin or guilt in his sayings and parables. Rather sin is seen as ignorance of the Order of the Universe. Sin is an imbalance, an accumulation of excess energy. And that excess accumulation of energy can be released by self-reflection and by self-purification. First, we review what we are doing and what we are thinking according to the Order of the Universe. With an empty mind, we should come back to the center—One Infinity—and say whatever we think and feel. "It was wrong to do thus and so. I now see I was greedy. I was selfish. I was fearful. I will be better next time. I will not cloud my mind over with heavy, rich food. I will share my happiness and joy with other people." Then heaven and earth will be very happy to hear that self-confession, and at the same time our delusions will disappear. This self-purification is taking care of sin.

Everything is governed by yin and yang, complemental and antagonistic forces, the laws of fullness and emptiness. If we are hungry for One Infinity, we shall be filled up with understanding of the Order of the Universe. If we are always giving away what we receive and keep ourselves a little bit empty, we will constantly be replenished by the infinite universe.

When we come into the Kingdom of Heaven, we see that everything is a bright, shining manifestation of universal order. There is nothing to be afraid of. When we have any kind of troubles or any difficulties, let us realize these are all delusions—just the inability of our little self to perceive the larger order. Let us accept them gratefully as challenges to raise our consciousness and bring us back to our real self. This is the truth by which all troubles can be healed. By making ourselves clean and clear, we can wipe away all our delusions and sufferings. Then we can realize that all our troubles and persecutions were nothing but the result of imbalance in our own way of life.

Concepts like guilt, sin, punishment, hell, and damnation are nothing but a product of learned conscience. If you are taught these things after you were born, then you will retain them and have a tendency to feel them the rest of your life. But they are not the real way the universe works. You should not have a guilty conscience or feel afraid. You should not feel guilt for not going into a dark church every Sunday. God is everywhere. God is in you. God is outside of you. There is nowhere where God is not to be found. Transmute persecutions into blessings and gratefulness and start to live in the Kingdom of Heaven.

70. Jesus said: "If you bring forth what is in you, it will save you. If you do not have it in you, that which you do not have will kill you."

Everyone must save himself or herself. Everyone is their own Messiah. A person of light like Jesus can point the way to the Kingdom of Heaven, but they can't make you live in it. They can't chew your food for you. They can't distribute your wealth. Only if you understand the Order of the Universe and apply its principles in daily life can you prosper.

When you desire something, the very thing that you desire will eventually destroy you. If you want a million dollars, that richness will destroy you. If you want fame, that fame will destroy you. If you want a very sweet wife or husband, that sweet spouse will eventually destroy you. Whatever you very strongly desire, by that you will be destroyed. That is the Order of the Universe.

So if you have fallen in love, and if you could marry that person, that is a cause for celebration. However, it could also be the greatest danger of your life. That person could be the cause of your destruction. It is far safer to marry your second choice. Slight difficulties will then always be around you. Such difficulties and perhaps disappointments would give you something to work on. That situation is much safer for your development.

The first choice is always what you want to have—your desire. And that strong desire will destroy you, because you will certainly abuse it. It is very interesting, isn't it? So take your choice in moderation. Take the second or third choice. Then you are safe.

Some people think this approach is too middle-of-the-road They think you would have greater joys the other way. Yes, you can choose that path if you like, but your sorrows will also be

greater, too. If you always take your first choice, if you always
fill yourself up, you will have big adventures. But you must be
careful of the consequences. That path is often a difficult one.
By seeking out the greatest adventure, you will always be in
great danger. You can choose that path if you like. But at the
same time, you must keep your wits about you. Otherwise you
may careen off the edge of many cliffs. The middle of the road
is a much safer place to be. If you wish to follow the path of
greatest adventure, you must eat simply in order to keep an
empty mind and maintain your best judgment.

**71. Jesus said: "I shall destroy this house, and no one shall
be able to rebuild it."**

This verse refers to Jesus's cleansing of the Temple in Jerusalem. Originally the Temple was a place to come and study the
Law or Order of the Universe. But over the centuries, understanding of the unifying principle of yin and yang—movement
and rest—and the perpetual cycle of Five Trees in Paradise was
lost as people departed more and more from the traditional way
of life including their dietary practice. By Jesus's time, a totally
dualistic mentality prevailed, dividing everything into good and
evil, sacred and profane, pure and impure, clean and dirty.

The house then that Jesus has come to destroy is not the
physical Temple itself but the delusional and dualistic view of
life on which it is based. This is what he is trying to pull down.
In the *Gospel of Mark*, at his trial Jesus is accused of saying, "I
will destroy this temple that is made with hands, and within
three days I will build another made without hands." [*Mark*
14:58] "The temple made with hands" includes the interpretations, doctrines, schools, and systems of the phenomenal world,
all of which have been made conceptually and artificially. "The
temple made without hands" is the infinite universe, the Kingdom of Heaven and natural order that is spread over the entire
earth. By cleansing the Temple of moneylenders and animal
sacrifices, Jesus is teaching people to cleanse themselves of de-

lusional, dualistic views and an imbalanced way of living and eating. Once they see the truth of his teaching, they will no longer be attracted to conceptual doctrines and unnaturally treated food. They will return to practicing the universal law of nature and the universe and see no need to rebuild the shattered temple of their ignorance.

72. [Someone said to him:] "Tell my brothers to divide my father's property with me." He said to him: "O man, who made me a divider [over you]?" He turned to his disciples and said to them: "For my part, I am not a divider, am I?"

Luke gives a more complete version of this passage: "And one of the company said unto him, Master, speak to my brother, that he divide the inheritance with me. And he said unto him, 'Man, who made me a judge or a divider over you?' And he said unto them, 'Take heed, and beware of covetousness: for a man's life consisteth not in the abundance of the things which he possesseth.'" [*Luke* 12:13-15] Jesus then goes on in Luke's account to teach the parable of the rich man who decided to store everything up for himself but who died that night (see *Saying* 63).

Again Jesus is teaching the Order of the Universe. The basic principle of return to One Infinity is unity and synthesis. Dividers are anyone with an overly analytical and dualistic mentality. They include specialists, experts, and others who see the parts but not the whole. They also include those who identify themselves as capitalists or communists, spiritualists or materialists, or followers of Caeser or the Temple. Those who divide everything and take for themselves are still stuck in a fragment of the spiral of physicalization. They are destined themselves to be sick, unhappy, and suffer until they overcome their attachment to ephemeral, fragmentary things. But those who seek One Infinity, those who have entered the Kingdom of Heaven and are on the return spiral of spiritualization, they will share and cooperate with others, in turn receiving whatever they need from the endless Order of the Universe. Jesus is speaking as a representative of this eternal, infinite being (Me). He is seeing the whole and acting from oneness.

73. Jesus said: "The harvest is great, but the laborers are few. Therefore, entreat the Lord to send out laborers into the harvest."

The harvest is realizing One Infinity, the great benefits and prosperity that come from consciously following the Order of the Infinite Universe. The seekers, or laborers, are few. The majority of people are not harvesting. Jesus is encouraging people to come out and partake of this great blessing.

In sending the disciples out on their own to teach, Jesus further teaches them that even though they are small in number, they can change the world. From a small seed, a mighty harvest results. A tiny amount of leaven causes the whole loaf to rise. This is the Order of the Universe—the logarithmic spiral that governs human affairs and social teachings as well as the natural world.

In a verse preserved by the early Church Father Irenaeus, Jesus is quoted as saying, "A grain of wheat will produce ten thousand heads, and every head will have ten thousand grains, and every grain will produce ten pounds of fine clean flour. And other seeds, fruits, and grass will produce in corresponding proportions." [Irenaeus, *Heresies* v. 33. 3]

The universe in which we live, as we know through our modern knowledge, is expanding constantly. One seed produces hundreds of seeds; hundreds of seeds produce thousands of seeds; thousands of seeds produce millions of seeds. "One grain, ten thousand grains" is the natural order and work of life.

When we receive one piece of bread or one bowl of rice, we receive enough energy to produce thousands of pieces of bread, or thousands of bowls of rice, and return that energy to those who nourished us in addition to many thousands of people. When we learn anything useful, we naturally distribute it to everyone around us. Give, give, and endlessly give is the most important principle of life, especially in the course of our spiritualization. By giving, we make ourselves happy and bring happiness to thousands of people. When we eat, we must distribute whatever we take in. If we do not do this, we cannot eat any further. Life is receiving and giving; and the more we give, the more we receive. When we keep ourselves busy from morning to evening, day and night, with the practice of the spirit of "one grain, ten thousand grains," we are living together with the expanding universe. Keeping this spirit is the essential way to live in the Kingdom of Heaven and realize endless peace and happiness.

74. He said: "Lord, there are many around the well, but none in the well."

Everyone is seeking One Infinity—the source of eternal health, happiness, and peace—but no one is drinking from its well. The clear water of truth is always available to refreshen and nourish us. But we prefer to go thirsty or drink from stagnant waters. Jesus is sighing over how ignorant and afraid people are. They are so attached to their relative worlds and illusions that they cannot see the truth in front of them.

75. Jesus said: "Many are standing by the door, but solitary ones are they who will enter the wedding chamber."

This verse continues the theme that many are called, but few are chosen. Many people are hanging around the door to eternal life, but only a few have taken it upon themselves to seek One Infinity and practice its endless order.

The bridal chamber is the Kingdom of Heaven. The bride and bridegroom are yin and yang. The solitary ones are those who can make yin and yang one, those who know the unifying principle, those who can turn sickness into health, sorrow into joy, war into peace. They will discover and live in the Kingdom of Heaven.

76. Jesus said: "The Kingdom of the Father is like a merchant who received merchandise and found a pearl. That merchant was wise. He sold the merchandise, and he bought the one pearl for himself. For your part, seek for the treasure without end which abides where no moth enters to consume and no worm destroys."

The pearl of great price is One Infinity. Once again, as in the parable of the big fish, Jesus is telling his disciples to seek the most valuable thing—an understanding of the Order of the Universe. This Order is eternal, invincible, unchanging. It does not decay or die like things of the relative world. Whoever acts from this place will find eternal life.

77. Jesus said: "I am the Light that is above them all. I am the Whole. The Whole came forth from Me, and the Whole returns to Me. Cleave a piece of wood, I am there. Raise the stone, and you shall find Me there."

In this passage, Jesus is acting as a representative who has been manifested by God or One Infinity. Everything in the manifested world—the Whole—came from the absolute world—from Me. Infinite order is to be found in wood, in stones, and in common everyday things. In equating himself with the universal Light, Jesus is identifying himself with the unifying principle, not with the popular expectation of the Messiah. Everyone is a person of light, if he knows about himself.

78. Jesus said: "Why did you come into the wilderness? To see a reed blowing in the wind? And to see a man clothed in soft garments? [Behold,] your kings and your powerful ones are those who are clothed in soft [garments] and yet they will not be able to know the truth."

During Jesus's day, many people went to the desert to listen to prophets such as John the Baptist and practice austerities with communities such as the Essenes. They believed that fasting,

prayer, and celibacy would lead to truth. Persons who had re-
nounced ordinary life were likened to reeds shaken by the wind.

The wilderness also attracted kings and rich merchants, who
came to do penance for their sins and give alms to the poor. The
Pharisees, in particular, were known as the men "clothed in
smooth garments."

What Jesus was trying to say was this. You have come to this
world, being born as human beings, and you see many things
going on around you. Some people are denying the body. Others
are indulging it. Ordinarily people don't live in the desert. They
have come out to the desert because they don't know the truth.
They are imbalanced. On the one hand, the spiritual seekers are
concerned only with things of the nonmaterial world. On the
other, the kings and great ones are concerned only with things of
the material and relative worlds, which are all ephemeral. Neither group can ever unify the nonmaterial and material worlds.

In this verse, Jesus is advising his disciples to avoid extremes.
Too much restriction of the body and mind is as bad as too much
comfort and license. Truth is to be found everywhere, in the
cities as well as in the wilderness, among the meek as well as the
powerful. The Kingdom of Heaven embraces both the material
and nonmaterial or spiritual worlds.

This verse can also be looked at as referring to life as a whole.
"Why are you born into this world—this wilderness?" Jesus
asks, "Did you come to become a scholar, a businessman, a
president and gain fine things? Such people don't know life and
ultimately perish away. What is your true purpose?"

**79. A woman from the crowd said to him: "Blessed is the
womb that bore you and the breasts which suckled you." He
said to [her]: "Blessed are those who have heard the word of
the Father and have truly kept it. For the day will come
when you will say: 'Blessed is the womb which has not conceived and the breasts which have not given suck.'"**

Once again, Jesus is hailed on his travels around the country as
the Messiah who will miraculously deliver people from their

troubles. In this verse, he is shaking his head and telling the woman that he is not the savior of popular expectation. He reproaches her to the effect: "I cannot save you from your difficulties. I am not an all-seeing, all-powerful emissary from above. Your salvation lies in understanding and observing the Order of the Universe." Praise One Infinity and the energy from the universe which nourishes you—"the womb which has not conceived and the breasts which have not given suck." Life is full of difficulties. Unless you know, practice, and appreciate this wonderful order that nourishes and sustains all, you will experience more and more suffering as a result of your ignorance and end up cursing life.

In the second sentence of this verse, the Greek term for "word" is *logos*. Logos is usually defined as word, principle, reason, or order. In the New Testament, its most famous usage is in the *Gospel of John*: "In the beginning was the Word (Logos), and the Word (Logos) was with God, and the Word (Logos) was God. . . . And the Word (Logos) was made flesh." [*John* 1:1,14] Generations of Christians have interpreted this in theological terms. They equate the Word of God with Jesus Christ (i.e., the Messiah). They believe that as the only begotten Son of God, Jesus incarnated into the flesh to save the world.

The real meaning of *logos* is more like wave or vibration. In the beginning, One Infinity gave rise to yin and yang. In turn, yin and yang produced energy and vibration, including light and sound. This energy—known as *ki* in Japanese and as *rauch* in Hebrew—was likened to wind, to breath, and to the universal sound that underlies all speech.

The actual pattern of all vibration and energy is spirallic. When Jesus uses the concept *logos*, he is using it in this sense. The "word of the Father" is the Order of the Universe. *Logos* is the logarithmic spiral. The word "logarithmic" comes from the same source. In our terms, we can say that *logos* is the unifying principle—an understanding of yin and yang, the spirallic laws of change and harmony. In Chinese Bibles, *logos* has traditionally been translated as the Tao.

Applying this interpretation, the verses are easy to understand

124

Figure 18. The Logos or Logarithmic Spiral.

Course of physical
and material
manifestation

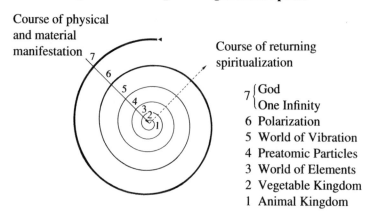

Course of returning
spiritualization

7 { God
    One Infinity
6 Polarization
5 World of Vibration
4 Preatomic Particles
3 World of Elements
2 Vegetable Kingdom
1 Animal Kingdom

in light of our diagram of the universal Spiral of Life *(see* Figure 18). "Blessed are those who have heard about the spirallic Order of the Universe and kept it in truth." "In the beginning was the Logarithmic Spiral, and the Logarithmic Spiral was made flesh." Jesus is just one manifestation of the spiral. Everyone is an incarnation of the *Logos* or Word of God.

80. Jesus said: "He who has known the world has found the body, and he who has found the body, of him the world is unworthy."

The world is not the earth or natural world around us. It is the world of delusions and fragmented understanding. Someone who is acting from this level has found only fleeting happiness and wealth.

What is the body? We have organs, bones, tissues, and so on. If we take all these out, "I" doesn't exist. The same way, if we remove the earth, sun, and universe, we wouldn't exist. The world is our external body. Who am I? Where am I? I am within and without. Everything is I. I am all. The body is not solid or material. As modern physics has shown, we are largely empty space. Even our atoms appear as much as streaming waves as solid particles. Every day energy is coming in, including air, sound, light, vibration, and food. Then energy is discharged constantly through urination, bowel movement, respiration, perspiration, and daily activity. We are open, not closed. Infinity comes in, condenses for awhile, and then leaves.

The body itself is not bad or impure. It is a manifestation of the infinite universe. What is limiting, however, is to regard the body as solid and permanent. Jesus is saying that people who become attached to the body, or the sensory level, never really develop their consciousness or spirit.

But whoever has found the order of change and harmony will enjoy lasting life and prosperity. He or she who understands the health and sickness of the body will not be attached to their difficulties and sufferings or the delusional world and its ephemeral rewards. They will acquire enduring health and happiness and nourish their consciousness or spirit. They are worthy of experiencing a greater realm—eternal life in the Kingdom of Heaven.

81. Jesus said: "He who has become rich, let him reign, and he who has power, let him abandon it."

By "rich," Jesus means rich in understanding, not rich in material goods. He who understands the Order of the Universe is qualified to govern. He knows the laws of change and harmony—yin and yang—and can guide society to greater health, happiness, and peace. On the other hand, he who is materially wealthy and powerful must continually distribute or give away his wealth and power to others. Otherwise, he will lose everything in the natural course of life as fullness turns into emptiness, and emptiness turns into fullness.

82. Jesus said: "He who is near to Me is near to the fire, and he who is far from Me is far from the Kingdom."

As in Verses 10 and 16, the fire here is the burning desire for eternal truth, for knowledge of One Infinity and the universal order of change. Whoever has such a flame in their mind or heart is near to Jesus. Whoever lacks such a spirit is far from realizing eternal life. Fire may also represent the energy of the whole universe.

83. Jesus said: "The images are revealed to man, and the light within them is concealed in the image of the light of the Father. He will reveal himself, and his image is hidden by his light."

In this and the following two verses, Jesus is commenting on the well-known passage in *Genesis* where Adam is said to have been created in the "image" and in the "likeness" of God. "And God said, Let us make man in our image, after our likeness. . . . So God created man in his own image, in the image of God created he him; male and female created he them." [*Genesis* 1:26–27] The Greek word for image is *eikon* from which the English word *icon* is derived.

More practically speaking, what is this "image?" It is each person's universe. God has made man "in his image." That means that God made our body just as the universe (*see* Figure 19).

It happens in this way: there are millions and billions of stars in our galaxy. The Milky Way envelops the earth, and there are many constellations within its stream of stars. While the earth rotates on its axis and orbits the sun, we receive the vibrational influence of endless stars coming in. The influence from one side forms the human spinal column and vertebrae. The influence from the other side forms the digestive organs. The natural electromagnetic charge between clusters of stars causes the charge between the organs, including our heartbeat. So our body is nothing more than the universe's condensed form, reflecting the contraction and expansion of yang and yin.

When we sleep, even though it is cloudy and rainy, radiation from the stars is coming down to us, revitalizing our organs and

Figure 19. The Image of God.

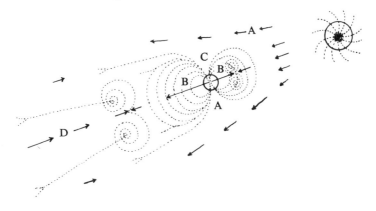

As the earth (C) rotates, electromagnetic orbits are generated and formed around the earth. Incoming solar wind (A) from the sun and the centripetal force from peripheral space (D) collide with the centrifugal force generated by the earth's rotation (B), and form a humanlike aura of electromagnetic or plasmic energy around the earth. Human beings may thus be said to be formed in the image of God or the Infinite Universe.

our bloodstream. The stars in the northern sky, situated more to the periphery of our galaxy, influence our head and brain. The stars in the southern sky, which are more toward the center of the Milky Way, influence the sexual organs. Our body is, therefore, nothing but a microcosm of the universe. The external universe, or the stars and constellations, is the expanded form. The internal body, or the organs, is the condensed form. The inside is yang, the outside is yin. The difference between the outside universe and the inside body is only one of yin and yang. They are both manifestations of One Infinity, but one is the centrifugal manifestation, the other is the centripetal manifestation. Like all phenomena in the infinite universe, human beings are fashioned according to the laws of spirallic order. Our spirallic structure is created in the image of God—the infinite spirallic universe.

Where do images come from? You remember something that happened ten or twenty years ago. An image arises in your mind. The same thing occurs if you go forward in time. You hold an image of the future. Our minds are constantly receiving vibration and waves, somewhat like a TV transmitter. When we receive, we translate or interpret into patterns, images, and sounds. A dog has dog consciousness and interprets these images in a dog way. A plant has plant consciousness and interprets them in a plant way. We interpret according to our human quality, capacity, and structure.

Everything has consciousness. The universe itself is formed of multiple levels of consciousness. Consciousness is governed by yin and yang. Sometimes it is active, other times it is resting. Sometimes it is up, other times down; sometimes positive, other times negative; sometimes excited, other times depressed. Consciousness is always moving. The origin of consciousness is beyond image or thought. The appearance of phenomena gives rise to consciousness. Each individual interprets differently, but the source is the same. How we interpret the images depends on the quality of our being. If our physical condition is healthy and our minds are clear, clean, and empty, we can interpret fully. Like a clear sky, we will perceive things as they really are: shining, radiant, endless. However, if our physical condition is bad, our mind will be cloudy. Like clouds in the sky, we will see only dark, gray, threatening shapes. These we call delusions. These can cover up our whole sky. We soon forget the beautiful infinite blue above and the bright radiant sun within.

Modern life is governed by delusions. Modern agriculture, medicine, science, education, government, and other institutions are all based on a dualistic view of reality. We are attached to the strange, dark shapes of our own creation and act upon those attachments.

Life is consciousness. A healthy human being freely creates clouds and images endlessly, enjoys those, and then erases them. Hanging on to these images is attachment and leads to suffering.

The bridge connecting the Big I and the small i is consciousness (*see* Figure 20). In the *Gospel of Thomas*, Jesus is trying to explain this. Over and over again, he is telling his students: "I

Figure 20. The Bridge of Consciousness.

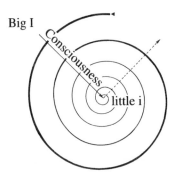

am the Infinite One, Big I. You are the Infinite One, Big I. Act
from that place. Everything is a manifestation of One Infinity.
There is no good or bad. All things are complemental. Everything is one." But the disciples are interpreting his words according to their own condition and image. Their universe is so
cloudy they cannot understand what he is trying to say. Jesus is
endlessly patient. He knows that it may take time to feel the
Infinite Self. You have to eat well and meditate and experience
many things.

"The images [of the relative world] are revealed to man, and
the light within them is hidden in the image [*Logos*: Logarithmic
Spiral] of the light of the Father [One Infinity]." This means that
without the keys of yin and yang, we cannot understand life. We
cannot understand the changing Order of the Universe around
us. We see wonderful shapes, sizes, colors, and sounds but not
the universal process of spirallic change that governs their appearance and disappearance. There is also the sense that we have
created a false image of the One, and by idolizing that image
have departed further from the true light of understanding.

"He [One Infinity] will reveal himself [in countless images],
and his image [*Logos*: Logarithmic Spiral] is hidden by his
light." This means that we are so dazzled by the beauty of the
infinite universe that we forget its marvelous order. The King-

dom of Heaven or Paradise is all around us, but we don't see it because of our own cloudy images.

84. Jesus said: "When you see a likeness of yourself, you rejoice. But when you see your images that came into being before you and neither die nor are visible, O how much will you bear!"

Our likeness is our self-image or social image. Many of us imagine that we are solid, upright, and respectable, and we delight in the face we present the world. We rejoice in the awards, recognition, and spiritual merit we have attained. Or sometimes our self-image is very poor. We are burdened by guilt, regrets, and failure. All these are just appearances, Jesus is telling his followers. The real world of absolute, invincible truth includes things far beyond anything you have experienced. It includes the images of yin and yang, the Five Trees in Paradise, and other waves and vibrations that preceded you in the Spiral of Life (*see* Figure 24). When you wake up to the marvelous Order of the Universe, especially the unmanifest realms of the sixth and seventh heavens, you will marvel at discovering your real infinite self, the you that is beyond space and time. Then you will be truly ashamed at your past attachment to your little self and the ephemeral things you chased after.

85. Jesus said: "Adam came into being from a great power and great wealth, and yet he did not become worthy of you. For if he had been worthy, he [would] not [have tasted] death."

Adam and Eve lost paradise by eating from the Tree of Good and Evil. They were children of a great power and wealth—One Infinity—but ate inappropriate food, became dualistic in their way of thinking, and experienced big difficulties. Because they forgot their eternal origin and destiny, their family declined. Because of their attachment to the relative world, they experienced suffering and death. You can be higher than Adam and Eve by observing the way of eating and the unifying principle. You can attain eternal life.

86. Jesus said: "[The foxes have] their [holes] and the birds have their nests, but the Son of Man has nowhere to lay his head and rest."

In the New Testament, this saying is prefaced by the appearance of a scribe who wants to follow Jesus (see *Matthew* 8:20 and *Luke* 9:58). He tells the young man that life on the road with him will not be easy. There will not be any of the usual comforts of home. If he is willing to live without attachments to home and family, he is welcome. The work is great, the laborers are few. Turning modern civilization from its disastrous course will consume all their time and energy. As free human beings, they will be so busy restoring order to society that they will have no time to rest.

In comparing himself to foxes and birds, Jesus is also reminding his listeners that human beings have a higher purpose than the animals. At birth, human beings have completed the Spiral of Physicalization and are ready to begin their return journey to the infinite. Their goal is to develop their consciousness and spirit. Birds and animals, on the other hand, are still physicalizing themselves. They are perfecting their sight, hearing, smell, movement, and other physical abilities. One day they will become human beings and begin the Spiral of Spiritualization. But until then, their home is on the earth. They have their holes and nests, their habits and attachments.

The problem is that many people are behaving more like animals than human beings. They are not eating whole grains and other food appropriate for the free, unrestricted development of human consciousness. They have become earth-bound and attached to the transient things of this world. They are regressing back to previous stages of evolutionary development. Natural free human beings are always refining their consciousness and spirit, never resting until they have reached their true home, One Infinity.

In the New Testament. Jesus refers to himself as the "Son of Man" more than any other term. It simply means a free human being—a son or daughter of the infinite universe.

87. Jesus said: "Wretched is the body that depends upon a body and wretched is the soul that depends upon them both."

Body and soul are not opposed. They are just different manifestations of energy. The body is condensed spirit; the soul is an expanded form of the body. As we have seen, the universal process of life involves constant transformation of energy from one state into another. A natural free human being is someone who understands their relation and can freely adapt to all circumstances as the Spiral of Life unfolds.

In contrast, someone who does not understand the Order of the Universe sees body and soul as antagonistic rather than complementary. Some modern scientists will accept as reality only that which is measurable to the senses and ignore the world of vibration and spirit. On the other hand, some religious seekers will 1) devaluate the body altogether and honor only the soul or 2) they will say the health of the body depends entirely on the soul. All of these approaches are one-sided and will inevitably lead to sickness and suffering.

Contemporary medicine, for example, has been unable to stem the tide of cancer, mental illness, AIDS, and other degenerative and immune-deficiency diseases because it is entirely dependent on physical methods of observation and treatment. On the other hand, many psychological and spiritual approaches emphasizing mind control and prayer to the exclusion of food, exercise, and other more physical methods are equally unsuccessful. Only when the dynamic relation of body and soul is understood and practiced—such as in daily cooking according to the Order of the Universe and in eating with a calm, peaceful mind—can epilepsy, cancer, and other forms of wretchedness be relieved.

88. Jesus said: "The angels and the prophets will come to you, and they will give you what is yours. For your part, give to them what you have, and say to yourselves: 'When will they come and take what is theirs?'"

Everyone knows of prophets—those who can foresee the Order of the Universe—but not everyone knows of angels and of devils.

There are two kinds of people in society (*see* Figure 21). Having started his life within and from One Infinity, "A" is on the way to becoming human, proceeding toward physical and material achievement, while "B" has already accomplished this and is on her way toward mental and spiritual development, returning to One Infinity.

Figure 21. Complementary/Opposite Courses of Human Development.

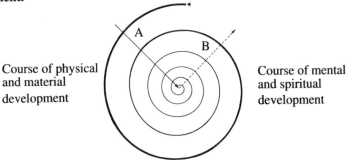

Course of physical and material development

Course of mental and spiritual development

One person is going one way, the other person is going the other way. "A" says to "B," "You are going the wrong way." "B" says to "A," "No, you are going in the wrong direction." Everyone's direction is right. Even though "A" is egocentrically and selfishly gaining, destroying others' happiness, gaining only for himself and his own benefit, his course will change eventually, and he will start to distribute to others. If he doesn't overcome his arrogance, then he will be destroyed by the Order of the Universe. His journey will suddenly end and his adventure on this planet will be over. Perhaps because he is overweight or because of cancer or AIDS. Perhaps he will be destroyed by some envious competitor or so-called enemy. The Order of the Universe is very amusing and very wonderful.

If you know the whole Order of the Universe, then for you there is no enemy and no difficulties. Everything is your teacher. Perhaps you have had some very sad experience with your parents or with a teacher or with a friend or some other people. But they are the real teachers. Without them, you could not learn what society is, what human life is, and what is your judgment. So they are the real teachers. We must appreciate them. Jesus said that if you are struck on the left cheek, you should turn the right one. He was trying to express the same thing. The more we are hammered, the more we can grow. If among you, you have a friend who uses only sweet words—"you are wonderful, you are beautiful, you are wise"—he may be a devil. If you have a friend who uses bitter words to you "you are no good, you should correct yourself"—he may be an angel for you. If you do not feel that way, it is because of your limited concept or image.

There is another meaning to devil. A devil not only accuses others and causes suffering but is someone who suffers—the person about whom we exclaim. "Oh, poor devil!" Real human beings are very rare. Few escape the physical, psychological, and spiritual pits of dualism. Most people are actually devils, and their hells are those of their own creation. How can we escape becoming a devil? Not, as many think, by confessing our sins and becoming an angel. This, again, is dualistic. Everything in this universe has two sides: nothing is totally pure, and the darkest thing will easily become the lightest. If we see a very big devil, we should be prepared to find him turn into a very good angel. Whatever has a front has a back: the bigger the front, the bigger the back. Japan was destroyed in the last world war, but without this destruction she could not have built the economy she has today and would not have the chance to make the self-reflection she has done. Japan has decided not to wage war in the future; without the bombing of her cities, this resolution would never have been made. Before we know it, our troubles have become our friends. And then, without devils, how could we know of angels? Life would become very stale. Your good character would never be appreciated in this sort of world.

If you want to be a devil then, become the biggest devil that you possible can. Not the sort of devil that we find at the lowest level, the hungry devil, the slave to money, power, fame, pleasure, knowledge. Push your egotism as far as it will go and aspire to become the greatest seeker of truth, justice, and love in the universe. If you do this, you must become the greatest angel, for neither angel nor devil exists at the extremity of development. For the free man or woman who is beyond dualism there is nothing stable or fixed. Knowing the laws of change, they can transmute hate into love, sickness into health, and devilishness into beatitude and back again.

This is the universal background to this verse. By angel, Jesus does not mean just a heavenly being with wings. In the first sentence, Jesus says, "The angels and the prophets will come to you and they will give you what is yours." By this he means everything that happens to you is fair and just. Whatever you receive—good or bad—is a manifestation of the Order of the Universe. You are your own savior—or destroyer.

There is also the use of angel in the usual sense. Angels, prophets, and other superior beings will appear before you—in church, on books, on TV—but the place they come from and the source of their inspiration—One Infinity—is also available to you.

"For your part, give to them what you have, and say to yourselves: 'When will they come and take what is theirs?'" Here Jesus is telling his disciples to act as a representative of One Infinity. Help and guide others, especially false prophets, fallen angels, angels, angels-in-training (devils). Everyone needs love and care. Always be prepared to act from your higher self. You and they are one. What is theirs, is yours, and what is yours is theirs.

Unfortunately, this understanding of angel and devil was lost. In the early Church, Jesus was turned into the risen, perfect Christ. Naturally the image of the fallen, imperfect Devil, or Antichrist, came out to make balance. Over the centuries, millions of people—Jews, Christians, Moslems, and others—have been thrust into hell on earth because of such cloudy thinking and delusions. To return to Paradise, we must recognize all apparent oppositions as part of a larger harmonious order.

89. Jesus said: "Why do you wash the outside of the cup? Do you not understand that he who made the inside is also he who made the outside?"

This is one of Jesus's strongest rebukes to the Pharisees. The Pharisees were the professionals, the upright, law-abiding citizens of the day. Compared to other groups in society, they were much more modern in their outlook. Yet even they couldn't understand why Jesus broke so many social rules and customs. They particularly attacked Jesus for eating with publicans and sinners and for not washing his hands before meals. On one such occasion, Jesus pointed to or picked up his cup and made this remark.

First, he is telling them that their display of cleanliness is superficial. It is external, decorative, impermanent. The dietary laws of that era were originally based on an understanding of the Order of the Universe but have degenerated into mechanical ritual. It is common sense to wash your hands before eating. But it is foolish to make this a universal law and punish offenders. In ignoring the rigid dietary laws, Jesus is saying that the spirit in which you eat is more important than what or how you eat. Of course, there were no hamburgers, French fries, refined flour, sugar, soft drinks, and artificial or chemical food then, so food quality was not as big a concern as it is today.

Secondly, Jesus is chastising his listeners for becoming dualistic. They think that "this is right," and "that is wrong." They have forgotten that everything has a front and a back; that if there is good, then there must be evil. And if there is beauty, there must be ugliness. These things cannot be separated from each other. The two sides of the cup represent all complementary/antagonistic relations: inside/outside; front/back; man/woman; brightness/darkness; body/spirit; beauty/ugliness. He is teaching them that they have to embrace both sides. Once again he is showing them how to make the two one, and live in the Kingdom of Heaven.

90. Jesus said: "Come to Me, for My yoke is easy and My rule is light, and you shall find rest for yourselves."

Here too Jesus is acting as the representative of One Infinity—Me. Life is easy for those who follow or unite with—yoke themselves to—the Order of the Universe. The Kingdom of Heaven—My lordship—is based on love and understanding, not force and conflict. It is gentle. At the end of your journey back to One Infinity, you will find repose in the Seventh Heaven, the true Sabbath, your eternal home.

91. They said to him: "Tell us who you are so that we may believe in you." He said to them: "You interpret the face of heaven and earth, but he who appears directly before you, you know not, and you do not know how to interpret this moment."

The disciples continue to be astonished at Jesus's words. They wonder if he is a prophet or the expected Messiah. They want proof in the form of wonder-working or miracles. Jesus rebukes them. He tells them that the infinite universe—the face of the sky and of the earth—is miracle enough. "You want proof of what I say? Look at the wonderful, endless Order of the Universe. It is all around you, but you don't see it. You don't know how to appreciate life."

92. Jesus said: "Seek and you will find. But those things that you asked of me in former days, I did not tell you then. Now I desire to tell them, but you no longer seek after them."

Jesus laments that his followers have such little burning quest for the truth. Before he put off directly answering their questions so that they could discover the Kingdom of Heaven for themselves. But now he wants to talk about deeper things, but they are not interested.

93. [Jesus said:] "Do not give what is sacred to the dogs, lest they cast it on the manure-heap. Do not throw pearls to the swine, lest they make it [into refuse and trample you underfoot]."

Continuing the same theme, Jesus warns against teaching eternal truths to people with low judgment. They cannot understand universal order and will misuse or ignore the teachings or even turn them around to the detriment of the teacher.

94 Jesus [said]: "He who seeks shall find, and to him who knocks it shall be opened."

This *Saying* is a variation of #2 and #92. Whoever seeks One Infinity will find it, and whoever knocks on the door to the Kingdom of Heaven, it will be opened. They will enter into a new world of endless order, beauty, and freedom.

95. [Jesus said:] "If you have money, do not lend at interest, but give it to him who will not give it back."

Money here represents not just currency but any materialized object, dream, or desire. Do things for their own sake, not for profit. Profit itself is all right (see *Saying* #109), but attachment to profit is harmful. Lend help and money to people because you really want to help them and because it's the right thing to do.

Don't seek any reward. When you empty yourself, naturally you will become full again. This is the Order of the Universe, endless distribution, logarithmic accumulation and dispersal.

96. Jesus [said]: "The Kingdom of the Father is like a woman. She took a little leaven, hid it in dough, and baked large loaves [of bread]. Whoever has ears let him hear."

In this passage, Jesus compares the Kingdom of Heaven to a woman making bread. He is saying that the Order of the Infinite Universe is spirallic. Everything grows like a seed according to the laws of expansion and contraction. From beginning to end, everything develops in logarithmic progression. From a little leaven, endless loaves of bread are created. From the infinitesimally small, the infinitely great is produced. Whoever understands the laws of yin and yang that govern the universe can do anything.

97. Jesus said: "The Kingdom of the [Father] is like a woman who was carrying a jar full of flour. While she was walking on a road far from home, the handle of the jar broke. The flour spilled out behind her on the road. She did not know it, as she was not aware anything was wrong. When she arrived home, she put down the jar and found it empty."

In this verse, Jesus alludes to the ephemerality of life. Whatever we do, all of our achievements disappear in the end. Vanity of vanities, all is vanity. One Infinity is manifested in all phenomena, but at the same time One Infinity is nothing.

The passage also illustrates once again the spirallic laws of nature. He is not chiding the woman for being negligent so much as noting that the meal she was carrying was lost in an orderly way. First, a small amount trickled out, then as the mouth of the jar gradually widened, more and more meal was lost. By the end of her journey, it streamed out in large volume and was all gone.

The examples in this verse and the previous verse complement each other. One illustrates the spirallic development of fullness, the other of emptiness. Both show the alternating stages of contraction and expansion, of yang and yin. Since these are universal principles, endless morals or lessons regarding gain and loss can be drawn from each example regarding human conduct.

Further, both verses involve grain or grain products. The first deals with making bread, the second with transporting flour. Jesus may have uttered these words while handing out whole grain barley bread to his followers as he is frequently depicted doing in the New Testament. Jesus drew upon many such examples from ordinary, everyday life. He knew that entering the Kingdom of Heaven was inseparable from observing a healthy, balanced way of eating. Throughout the gospels, he is portrayed as providing both material and vibrational nourishment to his followers.

98. Jesus said: "The Kingdom of the Father is like a man who wanted to kill a powerful man. In his house, he drew the sword and thrust it into the wall, to find out whether his hand would remain steady. Then he slew the powerful one."

This is one of the most puzzling sayings in the *Gospel of Thomas*. Unless our intuition is sharp, the identity of the two men is not immediately clear. Who is the slayer and who is the powerful man he wishes to slay? What is the house he is in? What is the wall? What is the sword he draws?

The subject of the verse, the first man, is ordinary humanity—the disciples, you, me, anyone seeking to develop themselves. The powerful man whom he wishes to kill is his egocentric self, the small i which is constantly attached to the things of the ephemeral world.

In order to realize the Big I—the Kingdom of Heaven—he must deliver himself from this powerful inner adversary. The small i is very strong. It is always demanding attention.

"It's mine."
"I'm entitled to it."
"I have to have it."
"Just a taste won't hurt me."
"Everyhody does it."
"Nobody will notice."

The small self is also too concerned with its own comfort and welfare to think of others.

"I can't wait."
"I'm too busy."
"It's your own fault."
"That's life."
"Thank God, I didn't get caught."

Or if the small self thinks of other people, it does so for selfish reasons.

"I hope other people will notice me."
"This shows how virtuous and compassionate I am."
"This makes up for what I did to so and so."

And on and on this inner dialogue continues as the small i finds continual reasons, excuses, and rationales to justify its egocentric behavior.

The house then is our mind, our universe. The wall is the un-natural boundaries that we erect around ourselves. The wall is the illusory images we create, the delusional systems we follow. These cloudy visions and artificial ways of life are blinding us to the true bright, shining nature of reality all around.

The sword that will cut through these barriers is supreme and universal consciousness—spontaneous, free, natural thinking and acting in perfect harmony with the Order of the Universe. The sword is a traditional symbol of acting upon higher con-sciousness. When King Arthur pulls the sword from the stone it is not because he is physically strongest. It is because he is spiritually highest. In the New Testament, the Word of God is likened to "a two-edged sword" [cf. *Hebrews* 4:12]. The two-edged, or two-sided, sword is mastery of yin and yang.

The sword is our perfected consciousness or spirit. With this sword, we are able to cut through the wall of delusions and realize our true self.

Of course, the process of entering and living in the Kingdom of Heaven is itself spirallic. In reality, the Kingdom is always present. It is immediately accessible. There are stories of people who found it after experiencing some great insight, difficulty, or shock. Understanding or tasting it is what Zen practitioners call *satori*.

But practically, it takes time to fully live in the Kingdom of Heaven. It takes effort and hard work. It takes persistence to wake up, overcome our attachments, and see the world anew through the magical spectacles of yin and yang. It takes practice to cultivate humbleness and modesty. We have to steady our hand, stabilize our confidence, develop our faith. To do this, we have to eat very well, live simply and gratefully, and help others. We cannot do all this overnight. It's best to start slowly, just like the leaven in the dough when making bread. Then step by step, we will develop and find the way to greater freedom and consciousness. This is the natural order, contraction, expansion, contraction, expansion. Take the good with the bad, the joyful with the sorrowful.

The other way, the dualistic way, the modern way, seeks endless expansion and gain, without any accompanying loss or hardship. This way peters out—like the meal lost on the road. Because we are so attached to the end result—for example, a delicious cake—we are careless and don't secure the handle of the jar tightly on our way home from market. Or our mind is so clouded over with images of enjoying the cake that we fail to heed our intuition when the handle of the jar flies open and the meal starts to trickle out. Such thoughts are the powerful man, the real landlord of our minds for whom we labor and pay constant rent through such trifling reflections and attachments.

So if we want to live in the Kingdom of Heaven, it's best to start slowly. Rather than change all at once, change one thing at a time. Don't give up eating cake altogether. Switch to a better quality cake. Use whole wheat flour instead of refined white flour. Use honey or maple syrup instead of sugar. Then later on, as your body adjusts to more natural foods, you can further improve your baking. Use *kuzu* to thicken with instead of eggs. Use barley malt or rice syrup instead of honey or maple syrup. And instead of eating three slices of cake each time you bake, eat two. Then eat only one. Then eat only a modest-sized piece. In this way, through natural logarithmic progression, we automatically reestablish health and order in our life and return to harmony with our natural environment.

If you proceed too fast, there is a danger that the opposite result may happen. Your resolve to change your way of eating will disappear like the lost meal. The keys to the Kingdom will be lost, and until you experience some great insight, difficulty, or shock you may not have another opportunity to find them. This is the practical kind of lesson we can draw from Jesus's parables.

99. The disciples said to him: "Your brothers and your mother are standing outside." He said to them: "Those here who do the will of My Father, they are My brothers and My mother. They are the ones who shall enter the Kingdom of My Father."

Here Jesus is contrasting our universal parents—heaven and earth—with our biological family. Those who do the will of the Father are those who live with the Order of the Infinite Universe. All humanity appear as a family sharing the same origin, the same home on this earth, and the same destiny which is the endless returning progression to One Infinity.

In verses like this, Jesus is telling his followers to go beyond the emotional level of judgment, which seeks personal love and fulfillment. Everyone has parents. Almost everyone wants a family, a wonderful husband or wife, and wonderful children. It is very natural to love them and create a lovely home. But if we limit our love only to our parents or family, our consciousness remains very low. He is telling his listeners to ascend the ladder or Spiral of Spiritualization (*see* Figures 3 and 16). At the next highest level, the intellectual, we love knowledge and learning and devote our time and energy to interpreting the world around us. At the social level, we love society and seek to establish universal justice for everyone. At this level, we also love the environment and seek to harmonize with the world of plants, animals, rocks, and stars. At the philosophical level, we love truth and become concerned about the ultimate nature of reality.

At the top, when we reach supreme and universal consciousness, our love becomes infinite, eternal, unconditional. It embraces everything. One Infinity is our true parent, and those who follow its marvelous, endless order are our brothers and sisters.

100. They showed Jesus a piece of gold and said to him: "Caesar's men demand we pay taxes." He said to them: "Give to Caesar the things of Caesar, give to God the things of God, and give to Me what is Mine."

This is one of Jesus's most famous sayings. But Thomas records the phrase: "Give to Me what is Mine," which is not found in the regular gospels. Who is Caesar? Who is God? Who is Me?

Caesar is not just the Roman Caesar, the imperial ruler over ancient Israel whose face appeared on currency of that era. Caesar represents the relative world, the world of manifestation.

God is One Infinity, the origin and source of eternal life. God is the bright shining one, the light within and without all things.

Me is the unifying principle, an understanding and application of yin and yang.

In asking this question, the Pharisees are trying to trap Jesus. Because of their dualistic way of thinking, they want him to take sides and thus alienate either the Romans or the Temple authorities. But Jesus responds at a much higher level. The people are astonished at his answer because it satisfies and unifies everyone.

Jesus uses Caesar, God, and Me in the same way he uses Son, Father, and Holy Ghost in *Saying* 44. Caesar and Son refer to manifested things of this world (*see* Figure 22). Father and God refer to the endless source of life—One Infinity. The Holy Spirit and Me refer to the world of vibration and spirit connecting the material and nonmaterial realms.

Figure 22. The Eternal Process of Change: Jesus's View.

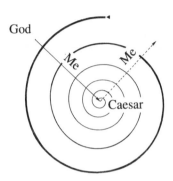

Here Jesus is acting as a representative of the Order of the Universe and therefore identifies himself with "Me" and "Mine." In *Saying* 44, Jesus said it is all right to blaspheme or ignore the Father and Son, but not the Holy Spirit or Order of the Universe. Similarly, here he implies that people can take or leave Caesar and God, but they should be very careful to render "to Me what is Mine." In other words, they can do as they like in respect to following learned conscience—obeying the Roman authorities and observing Temple customs. But universal conscience cannot be ignored. Harmonizing with the laws of nature and the infinite universe leads to happiness, freedom, and eternal life.

Another term Jesus frequently uses is Son of Man. It is very different from the term Son. Son represents any manifested reality, including ordinary human beings. Son of Man signifies a person who has attained universal consciousness, someone who understands and knows how to apply yin and yang and someone who dedicates his human life in working for the health and hap-

piness of all people. Such a person has become one with the
Order of the Universe and can act as a representative of "Me."

Except for Thomas, Jesus's followers did not understand his
answer. Later when the other gospels were composed, the saying
"and give to Me what is Mine" was left out.

**101. [Jesus said:] "He who does not hate his father and his
mother in My way cannot be My [disciple]. And whoever
does [not] love his [father] and his mother in My way cannot
be My [disciple], for my mother [gave me birth], but my true
Mother gave me Life."**

As in *Saying* 99, Jesus is encouraging his students to go beyond
the emotional level to higher levels of consciousness. By hate
and love, he means more like attachment and nonattachment. He
is contrasting biological parents with spiritual parents. Our individual mother and father give us birth, take care of us, and prepare us to enter society. We should love and respect them un-
conditionally. But our parents do not always know or apply the
Order of the Universe. They have limitations that we have to
recognize. In some cases, we may have to disregard their com-
mands or wishes and follow our own intuition and dream. It may
be that we teach them the way of life and show them how to
recover their health and happiness.

Also our real origin or parent is the endless universe. It is our
true Father and Mother. From that source, we receive eternal
life. This is what Jesus is trying to say.

**102. Jesus said: "Woe to the Pharisees, for they are like a
dog sleeping in the manger. He neither eats nor allows the
oxen to eat."**

The Pharisees—modern people in general—are ignorant of the
Law or Order of the Universe. But they uphold all kinds of rules
regulating daily life. In this verse, Jesus is saying that the leaders
of society are not capable of guiding people—i.e., taking care of

the oxen. They are like a dog in the manger—an earnest, hard-working, well-meaning creature but one lacking in higher consciousness. They do not eat or nourish themselves on the Order of the Universe. Nor do they let the people—the oxen—eat and be free.

103. Jesus said: "Blessed is the man who knows at what hour the thieves will enter. He will awake and gather his [treasure] and be prepared before they arrive."

Here Jesus continues to exhort his disciples to follow an orderly life. Blessed is the person who knows the Order of the Universe. He or she knows how yin and yang—earth and heaven's forces—govern day and night. They know the appropriate time to eat, sleep, wake up, and carry out their daily activities. The robbers are whatever and whoever make us trapped into delusional worlds and spoil and take away our intuitive oneness with the infinite and its natural order. Our treasure is discovery of One Infinity and living with its endless order. His preparation is self-awareness, faith, and conviction of his eternal life as One with the infinity. If we are always mindful of that wonderful shining reality—gather our treasure—we will always be prepared with self-mastery when encountering temptation.

104. They said [to him:] "Come, let us pray today and fast." Jesus said: "What sin have I committed? Or in what way have I failed? When the bridegroom comes out of the wedding chamber, let people fast and pray."

The disciples are on the passive side. They are weak, slow, dull. Like many spiritual seekers, there is a tendency to fast, pray, and practice celibacy in order to make themselves stronger. They are followers. They are always looking for a leader to tell them what to do. They ask Jesus to lead them in these spiritual practices. He rebukes them for thinking in these terms. He tells them that there is an order to prayer and fasting. As we saw in *Saying* 14, by sin Jesus doesn't mean moral transgression. He means accumulation of excess energy—becoming too yin or yang. These penances are appropriate for someone who has violated the Order of the Universe, for example, someone who has eaten too much dessert and gotten a stomachache. They are also fitting for someone who has failed, for someone who has been defeated in some way. They have not finished their homework. They have been turned down for a date. They have not secured the contract. They have not produced a crop. The examples are endless.

You may fast if your condition is too yin like this, Jesus says. Your body is soft. Your mind is weak. Your *ki* is low. Strengthen yourself. Concentrate. Empty yourself. Become more yang. But don't ask me to lead you. I am already yang enough.

The bridal chamber is the infinite universe, the house of yin and yang. The bridegroom is yang, the force of contraction, heaven's incoming centripetal energy. The bridegroom coming out of the bridal chamber means becoming too yin. The yang force has diminished. Then is the time to fast and pray and make yourself stronger. When you are in harmony with the Infinite Universe, there is no need for austerities or special practices. Everything is natural, wonderful, spiritual, free. Enjoy yourself. Play endlessly. Eternal life is like this. It is a merry wedding feast, a never-ending banquet, a celebration. Sing, dance, be forever happy.

105. Jesus said: "He who knows father and mother shall be called the child of a harlot."

This appears to be part of a longer verse that has now been lost. It may have continued something like this: "But whoever knows My true Father and My true Mother shall be blessed."

In any event, these words continue a familiar theme. Jesus is contrasting attachment to parents, family, and things of the relative world with knowledge and free exercise of the infinite world and its order. Again what Jesus is trying to say is that by staying stuck at the lower levels of judgment, you will miss your true inheritance. You will sell or trade your eternal life for limited, fleeting things. Elevating your consciousness and becoming one with your true parents in heaven—One Infinity—is our universal birthright.

In his own life, from the time he wandered off as a boy and was discovered in the Temple by his parents, Jesus appears to have faced constant problems with his family. No doubt his parents and relatives wanted him to meet a nice girl and get married, become a successful carpenter, and raise a big family. They couldn't understand his burning desire to spread the teaching of eternal truth, help relieve people of their suffering, and try to correct the imbalances in modern society. They could only see the trouble he was bringing down on himself and their family. Of course, this view was very narrow. Jesus was coming from a much higher level of consciousness. He saw heaven and earth as his true parents. He saw all people as his family. This made for endless difficulties and misunderstandings. Jesus was very yang. Had his expression been less strong or had he lived longer and matured, he would probably have reconciled himself with his family.

106. Jesus said: "When you make the two one, you shall become children of man, and when you say: 'Mountain, move,' it will be moved."

This is another version of *Saying* 48. Jesus is saying that if you can apply yin and yang, you can move mountains. If you have faith in the Order of the Universe, you can do anything. Faith is different from belief. Believing means to accept something without understanding it, without knowing if it is true, without asking whether or not you should act upon that idea.

If you cannot understand something, then you can either try it out on yourself, and if you then think that it is good, you can believe it. If you think it is not good, then you should drop it. Or you can question it with why, why, why, until you understand it. Once you have reached understanding, then you can have faith.

That faith can direct your life. It can be the basis for real orientation. You can go with your own initiative. You become your
own master, your own messiah. You are a son of man, a daughter of humanity. As long as you "believe," you will be afraid.
You will be the slave of some master, some book, or some
teaching.

Instead of belief, we should foster faith. No one can come to
you and say, "Faith this." No one can do this. No one can force
you into faith. That is something you have to do for yourself.
That means that unless you really understand, you cannot have
faith. A teacher of life like Jesus can make you believe, by explaining this and that. But that is not his purpose, and that is why
he taught in parables and answered his disciples questions with
further questions of his own.

We can use his words and explanations as a means for understanding. But understanding is up to us. It depends upon eating
well, cultivating a modest and humble spirit, observing other
people, and encountering many situations and difficulties. In that
way your understanding can develop, and you can have a basis
for your faith to grow. Once you have learned for yourself, decided for yourself, understood for yourself, then your ideas will
never be shaken.

In the West, there is a proverb: "The fear of God is the beginning of wisdom." Many people take this to mean fear of a heavenly judge who metes out punishment to sinners. This is not the
meaning at all. The original saying comes from *Proverbs* 9:10 in
the Bible. Its intent is more like, "The fear of the Order of the
Universe is the beginning of wisdom." For example, if we eat
too many apples, we will get diarrhea. Or if we never eat any
apples or fruit, we may get tight and constipated. So we have to
be very careful of extremes, very respectful of natural order.
This is not really fear. It is more like understanding cause and
effect. It's entirely up to us which way we shall go and whether
we shall be well or sick, rewarded or punished. Also people tend
to forget the second half of the saying from the Bible. The full
sentence reads: "The fear of the Lord is the beginning of wis-

dom: and knowledge of the Holy [One] is understanding."
Clearly, the second part refers to God or One Infinity, while the
first part refers to the Law or Order of the Universe. A better
translation of the first part would be, "Faith in the Order of the
Universe is the beginning of wisdom," or "Respect for the Order
of the Universe is the beginning of wisdom."

There is another kind of fear. It is based on ignorance of God
or the Order of the Universe. Belief comes from this fear, deep
inside fear. Because of this fear, many people feel an inner lack
of centering, a deep frustration. They hear somebody say they
have a balm for this hurt, a nourishment for that hunger. So they
go to this new spiritual doctor, general, or politician, and they
believe what he has to say. This has happened frequently over
the past thousands of years. This kind of mentality creates societies of slaves. They are all slaves of their own fear, of their own
belief.

Instead of this, we act upon faith. We try to understand everything. Among Jesus's disciples, who was the person with the
spirit of *Non Credo:* I don't believe? Thomas. Doubting Thomas. He questioned everything. He questioned his teacher's
words. He questioned his friends' words. He questioned the
resurrection of Jesus. He said that until he could see for himself,
he would not believe. Alone among the disciples, Thomas had
true faith.

**107. Jesus said: "The Kingdom is like a shepherd who had a
hundred sheep. One of them, the largest, went astray. He left
behind the ninety-nine and sought for the one until he found
it. After all his hard work, he said to the sheep: 'I love you
more than the ninety-nine.'"**

In this parable, the big sheep is like the big fish in *Saying* 8 and
the pearl of great price in *Saying* 76. The sheep is a symbol of
the most valuable thing, One Infinity. The other ninety-nine
sheep stand for lesser things, the pleasures and attractions of the
phenomenal world. Like the faithful shepherd, we should not

hesitate to leave everything else behind to seek the greatest thing, the largest life—*macro bios*—the kingdom of infinite peace, endless happiness, eternal life.

This verse clarifies the relation not only between the One and the Many but also between the One and the Kingdom of Heaven. The One is not the Kingdom of Heaven. The Kingdom of Heaven creates One. The Kingdom of Heaven is totality, everything, the whole process of appearance and disappearance, being and nothingness.

In the Far East, the unnamed, unknowable absolute from which the One emerged is called the Tao. The *Book of Genesis* refers to it as the Void. In other traditions and religions, it is sometimes referred to as nothingness or infinite darkness.

The Kingdom of Heaven creates one, then two, then three, then everything—hundreds and millions of things. Then these dissolve back into One, and One dissolves back into nothingness. Then again One comes out, then two, then many. This endless motion, this endless order is the Kingdom of Heaven, the Tao. In this passage, the appearance and disappearance of the One is suggested by the straying of the sheep and its reunification with the flock (the many).

108. Jesus said: "He who drinks from My mouth shall become like Me and I will become [like] him. And to him, the hidden shall be revealed."

The disciples marvel at Jesus's expression and regard him as the Messiah or savior. They feel surrounded by enemies and see him as the deliverer of popular expectation. They are afraid of the Romans, the Temple authorities, the Pharisees, and the Zealots. They are afraid of disease, of poverty, of old age, of dying. They are afraid of Life.

Jesus is teaching them the unifying principle so that they can take charge of their own destiny. By making the two one, they can transform enemies into friends and lead a happy, peaceful life.

Let's take a look at this process. When confronted with an enemy, there are five general reactions. We can fight back, we can run away, we can surrender, we can be so confused, so cloudy, that we are unable to do anything at all, or we can change that enemy into our friend. The first four responses are all accompanied by fear. Only the last one brings lasting peace.

We must realize that our enemy is already our friend. He is our opposite, and because of this he can see things that we cannot. And he can do things that we cannot. But just intellectually thinking that we can learn and grow from our so-called enemy's example is not enough. We must really feel this and with deep gratitude be thankful to this person or this situation because it is by this that we grow.

How can we change our thinking to see that our enemy, including sickness, is our friend? We need the understanding of yin and yang. And we must begin to change ourselves instead of trying to change the enemy. If sickness comes, if difficulties arise, then these things are signals, warnings, angels reminding us that in some way we are living against the Order of the Universe. So if terrorists attack, or bacteria spread through your body, then immediately you must begin to change yourself. Then automatically, to this enemy your body and your condition are different. So the enemy loses ground to attack. In the same way, when bacteria start to create an infection, at that time you must change yourself. This means changing the quality of your blood. Then the bacteria can no longer live there. And how do we change our blood quality? By what we eat and drink.

"He who drinks from My mouth shall become like Me and I will become like him." By nourishing ourselves on the unifying principle and eating the same food, we develop the same consciousness. We become brothers and sisters of One Peaceful World. In the ancient world, it was widely understood that people who ate together developed the same dream, shared the same mentality and spirit. In the Middle East, soldiers who had shared a meal together were forbidden from fighting. For example, *The Talisman*, a historical novel by Sir Walter Scott,

154

opens with a European Crusader and a Saracen knight engaged
in mortal combat in the Holy Land. When their heavy armor is
knocked off, they recognize that they once ate together during a
truce. They immediately throw down their weapons, embrace as
brothers, and share a simple meal of bread and salt.

In Thomas's saying, there is the same idea. By eating together
and nourishing ourselves on One Infinity, we become friends
and comrades. We no longer need to divide ourselves into antagonistic groups of saviors/sinners, doctors/patients, masters/
disciples, friends/enemies. We are children of the same Father,
and by studying the Order of His Infinite Kingdom everything
will become plain and clear.

**109. Jesus said: "The Kingdom is like a man who had a
treasure [hidden] in his field but did not know it. After he
died, his son assumed ownership of the field. But he did not
know about it either and sold the field. The one who bought
it, while plowing, [found] the treasure. He began to lend
money at interest to whomever he pleased."**

Some people think that virtue is doing God's will or what in
our terms we call following the Order of the Universe. But you
cannot escape God's will or the Order of the Universe. So virtue
doesn't really exist. Just the fact that you exist is "virtue." But
there is still a difference. What kind of difference? Whether you
follow God's will or the Order of the Universe consciously or
unconsciously is the difference.

For example, suppose you eat plenty of hamburgers and
French fries and get a heart attack. That is following the Order
of the Universe. You can't escape from it. You take "this," and
"that" result will follow. But if you are following this Order of
the Universe unconsciously, the results that come are totally
unexpected. But when you know what you are doing, then you
anticipate and understand the result. That is the difference. By
consciously knowing what we are doing, we can change the
results. That is freedom. But people who follow the Order of the

Universe blindly, without knowing, have unexpected results. They don't know why things happen, why sickness comes, what brings on accidents. And they are anxious and frightened. And they cannot change these results. They cannot turn yin into yang, or yang into yin. When tragedy strikes, they go into a hospital and in many cases get worse, lose all they have, and die. But someone who knows yin and yang can restore balance. By applying the laws of change and harmony, they can treat underlying causes rather than symptoms. They can self-reflect, change direction, and find a lasting solution to their troubles.

This is the theme of this verse. The man who has a treasure in his field is someone who follows the Order of the Universe blindly. He is unconscious. He never found the treasure hidden in his field—One Infinity and its endless Order. Nor could he guide his son, and so his son also remained blind. But the man who bought their field was a seeker of truth. He was conscious. He didn't leave the field untended. He worked it, he plowed, he practiced changing directions, going first right, then left, going forward, then backward. He was able to apply the laws of yin and yang in his daily life. He found the treasure of eternal life. "He began to lend money at interest to whomever he wished." He profited from every experience, good or bad, and did whatever he liked. His prosperity grew logarithmically.

110. Jesus said: "He who has found the world and become rich, let him renounce the world."

This is similar to *Saying* 81. Whoever has succeeded in the material world must continually distribute his wealth and power. Otherwise, he will lose it unexpectedly. That is the Order of the Universe: gain, loss; fullness, emptiness. The only choice we have is whether we follow this consciously or unconsciously. If we give away our good fortune to others, we will continue to prosper. If we are not attached to power and control, more and more people will turn to us for help and guidance.

Sometimes, though, it is very difficult to influence others. We may even be persecuted. But if we are put into jail, no one can suppress our dream, our ideas, our spirit. Modern society killed Jesus, but Jesus's ideas still live on. In the same manner, our dream or ideas can live beyond any boundaries. The essential point is whether we are seeking material, physical success or seeking to understand the invisible, invincible Order of the Universe. When we pursue a spiritual dream, the product of our endeavors can last for thousands of years. But if we concentrate on building material civilization, then after only a few hundred years these things will decay. Lao Tzu was living in a small kingdom over which he was the curator. That kingdom has long disappeared, but the name of Lao Tzu and what he wrote still remains. The same thing is true with Moses and the other Jewish prophets. Their physical kingdom is gone, but their words and ideas still have meaning today. These people were spiritual, philosophical, so their expression still lives.

111. Jesus said: "The heavens and the earth will be rolled up before you, and he who lives [according to] the Living One shall see neither death nor fear, for as Jesus has said: 'He who finds himself, of him the world is not worthy.'"

When I was young, I was invited to visit a friend in the mountains of California near Bakersfield. My friend, Herman Aihara, was with me, and we were both very excited about the beautiful scenery. After supper, we were preparing for bed. My room was in the house, but Herman was to sleep in the shrine farther up the mountain. Herman felt very honored to be permitted to sleep in the shrine. He left with his blankets and candle, and I went to my room. I was brushing my teeth when all of a sudden I heard Herman anxiously rapping on the door. I let him in. "Michio, Michio," he blurted out. "A horrible thing is there! I can't sleep there!"

I went with him up the mountain to the shrine to see what it was that had disturbed my friend so much. As I entered the shrine, I saw nothing, until in the candlelight I saw on the wall a picture of Jesus hanging from the cross, suffering, bloody, tormented. I was so shocked. Of course, Herman cannot sleep there, I thought. I wouldn't be able to sleep there either. Some frightful spirit is coming from that picture.

What kind of mind or mentality could pray in front of such a picture? Instead of peaceful, merry, happy thoughts, there could be nothing but horror, shock, and guilt. Such representations of Jesus could only bring images of fear into your mind. Only thoughts of punishment could be engendered. Or perhaps revenge. This kind of mentality creates big trouble.

Naturally the Jewish people have long been persecuted because of such dark, cloudy images and expression. Naturally wars under the name of Christianity have been fought. Naturally hangings and other forms of execution under the guise of religion have been going on for centuries. Such horrible things have happened because people have become fixated or attached to the horrible aspect of the crucifixion.

This is the biggest issue of religion. Deep inside, many people harbor a horrible fear and hell. A natural free human being doesn't have this torment at all. Why do so many people, not just Christians, but also Buddhists, Taoists, Moslems, and many others, have horrible hells inside of them. Why do they want to suffer?

The problem facing humanity is how to release people from this hell, how to wipe out this illusion, this nightmare that they are eternally sinful and doomed to suffer. If people were released from this delusion, then they would become very happy. Unless we can cure this fear, there will be no happiness in the world.

This saying appears to be very apocalyptic. Like the *Book of Revelation*, it suggests images of the final judgment, the salvation of the righteous, and the destruction of the damned. But this is not Jesus's intent at all. That is a misreading, resulting entirely from our deluded imagination.

"The heavens and the earth will be rolled up before you." What does it mean? The heavens and the earth, as we have seen,

are the seven heavens, the Spiral of Life (*see* Figure 5 and 15).
They will be rolled up in your presence. That means in the
course of your long journey from One Infinity to manifestation
here on this earth and back again, you will experience all seven
heavens. They will roll up and unroll like a logarithmic spiral.

"[A]nd he who lives [according to] the Living One shall see
neither death nor fear. . . ." Those who are conscious of the Order of the Universe will pass smoothly from one level to another. They will not be afraid of death—birth into the next
level—nor will they be afraid of life—the other beings with
whom they share this marvelous journey.

"[F]or as Jesus has said: 'He who finds himself, of him the
world is not worthy.'" The reason they are not afraid is because
whoever knows his or her real self—One Infinity—will not be
attached to lesser things. The changing forms and fleeting pleasures of the six relative worlds will not interfere with the development of their consciousness. Their spirit will continue to grow
until it becomes one with Eternal Life itself.

Like Jesus and his disciples, macrobiotic friends can relieve
present-day incurable sicknesses such as heart disease and cancer. These things are relatively easy. Even various mental illnesses and AIDS can be reversed. But this deep, deep religious
fear, which is invisible, which most of us have, which is so horrible, we must learn how to cure. There again, it is nothing more
than the application of yin and yang. The unifying principle has
the answer and the cure for this problem. All we have to do is to
understand what it is, where the origin of our attachment to dark,
bloody images lies. Then we can find the cure. Definitely this is
related to the eating of animal food, to the same kind of thing
Jesus was trying to express when he freed the doves and other
sacrificial animals in the Temple and chased out the moneylenders who profited from this trade.

It is very important to change this pattern of eating. Eating
animal food, especially hard saturated fat and dietary cholesterol
such as found in meat, eggs, and poultry, creates a very narrow,
rigid mind. Such a mind has a hard time experiencing the verti-

cal world of vibration and spirit. It tends to remain at the horizontal level preoccupied with territoriality, possessions, and other material pursuits. Eating dairy food, as well as oily, greasy, sticky food in general, contributes to dependency and attachment. Feelings of gloom, despair, worthlessness, and guilt can arise from eating these kinds of food. Our minds and bodies become stagnant and sticky, and the bright, shining light of reality cannot come in or out.

Unless we are relieving suffering, then our teachings are as worthless as pouring water upon the dry sand. Endless teachings, endless words are nothing unless we can practice them and enable people to overcome their sicknesses and illusions. We must be able to erase this deep inner fear that so many people have. We can conceptually understand this problem. But we cannot get to the nightmare that haunts so many people. This is the biggest issue of religion. We must try to cure this fear, this feeling of original sin and guilt. This is the number one delusion in the whole world.

Closely connected with this is the feeling that we are saved and that other people are inherently evil and eternally damned. In society, this takes the form of apocalyptic thought: that our religion is the best, that God is on our side, and that our enemies will be destroyed in the final battle of good and evil. Many Christians think that Armageddon is approaching and that the legions of evil will be destroyed in a cataclysmic last war. Many in the East think that World Revolution is just around the corner and that communism will inherit the earth.

Dark, bloody images like these govern modern life in many capitals around the world. Millions and billions of lives on this planet weigh in the balance. Actually no such struggle between good and evil is taking place. Everyone must know that what is considered right and wrong, sin and guilt, is nothing more than their own one-sided view. It is nothing more than a cloudy image, a social delusion that has been maintained from generation to generation, and become bigger and bigger as the centuries have passed. Now is the time to be rid of this fear and see all antagonisms as complementary, to see all foes as friends, to turn all devils into angels. But we must learn how to do it.

112. Jesus said: "Woe to the flesh that depends upon the soul; woe to the soul that depends upon the flesh."

Separating life into flesh and soul, body and mind, and matter and spirit is a hallmark of modern dualistic thinking. In Jesus's day, materialists like the Sadducees denied the world of vibration and spirit and the needs of the soul. Spiritualists like the Essenes denied the material world and the needs of the flesh. These two tendencies are still very widespread in the world today. Many scientists and intellectuals deny the spiritual side of life that cannot be measured by the senses or other physical means. Many religious people overlook the health of the body and reject the material side of life that seems unrelated to the development of their consciousness and spirit.

In this verse, Jesus is cautioning against both of these types of one-sided thinking. As in *Saying* 29, he is saying that flesh and soul are interrelated. The body is an expanded form of the mind; the mind is a condensed form of the body. Matter and spirit are two sides of the same coin. They are manifestations of One Infinity. Unless we understand this relationship and how to balance yin and yang, the immaterial and material worlds, we will inevitably suffer. Those who depend only on sensory things will be unhappy when those things run their course. They will live their lives in darkness, unaware of the larger world of vibration and spirit within and around them. Those who depend only on the soul will be unhappy too, because the quality of their spirit is largely determined by how well they are able to harmonize with the natural world. They will live in darkness, unaware that their day-to-day physical health and vitality are guiding and shaping the quality of their consciousness and spirit.

The next life is a continuation of this life. And this life is something like an embryonic life toward birth into the next life. Our health, our judgment, and our behavior very largely depend upon the condition of our embryonic period, especially the food that our mother ate during pregnancy. In the same manner, our condition in the next world of vibration and spirit is largely dependent upon our development here in this life, especially our day-to-day eating. So when you live your life according to the demands of genuine conscience, then the next life is very simple. When you follow the dictates of the learned social conscience, and die with it, then the next life will be very difficult. The next life is not like this one with laws and regulations. The next life is governed by consciousness. Intuition leads, not power. So when you follow genuine conscience or the large self in this life, it is easy to make the transition. The principles will be applicable in the next life as well as in this life. But if you follow the learned social conscience or the small self, the adjustment will be very difficult.

113. His disciples said to him: "When will the Kingdom come?" [Jesus said:] "It will not come by expectation. No one will say: 'Lo, here it is,' or: 'There it is.' But the Kingdom of the Father is spread over the earth and men see it not."

Truth is universal. Truth is beyond time and space. It is everywhere and anywhere. The Kingdom of Heaven is not a life that will come someday. The disciples are thinking, "Salvation will come in the future." But it is not like that at all. The Kingdom of Heaven is here already. Our life on this planet is part of the Infinite Universe, and if we cannot change this earth into a paradise, we cannot do anything after our death. Many people, especially religious people, think that since we cannot find happiness in this relative world, then we shall find it in Paradise after death. This is schizophrenic thinking because after death or before death, we are always within the Kingdom of Heaven. The density of vibration may differ from one level—or heaven—to another, but the quality remains unchanged. That quality depends on our health and consciousness.

The Kingdom of Heaven is always here. Why cannot we see it? Because of our distorted vision. We are using certain colored eyeglasses. Why are our minds so colored? Because of improper eating of daily foods. Because of our conceptual education. If we eat the wrong way and are trained in the wrong method, our sight becomes blind or distorted. We see only illusions, fantasies, shadowy images. We do not see the clear, shining light of reality.

If we are eating properly and are studying the Order of the Universe, our sight will become clear, penetrating, and all-embracing. We shall discover that we are in the Kingdom of Heaven and have been all along. We are living in Paradise, only before we were not conscious of it. This Infinite Universe itself is the Kingdom of Heaven. It is the endless, immortal order governing all things. In spring, the trees burst forth with new life. In summer, they billow with deep green leaves. In autumn, they turn majestic colors and then fall to the ground. In winter, snow nestles on the empty branches. All seasons have their time and their beauty. The stars are constantly circulating overhead, sending us a steady shower of radiation. The sun and the moon are always in motion, giving us their energy. The wind eddies around us. The water nourishes our thirst. And all the animals, birds, and insects are thriving on the surface of this earth with us.

We are living in the Kingdom of Heaven every second of our lives. Governed by spirallic motion, everything is revealing the Kingdom. If we properly understand the laws of change and harmony, in every action and experience, including all difficulties and sufferings, we can see the wonderful Order of the Universe. We see that everything is within the Kingdom of Heaven and everything occurs by the same principles. This order proceeds continuously, and everything is proceeding toward harmony, always and forever. And yet we have forgotten this essential truth. We forget that the Order of the Universe, which leads and governs everything, is the tangible justice of the Kingdom of Heaven. Instead, we think that life is unfair and without order or meaning. We think that the Kingdom of Heaven is somewhere else, somewhere we can go to, something we can achieve as a reward for our good actions.

Why have we forgotten where the Kingdom of Heaven is? Why have we forgotten to marvel at nature and appreciate all forms of life, including all people? To remember these things and to have them in our minds at all times is the true character of natural free human beings.

114. Simon Peter said to them: "Let Mary leave us, because women are not worthy of Life." Jesus said: "Behold, I shall guide her and make her male, that she too may become a living spirit like you men. For every woman who makes herself male shall enter the Kingdom of Heaven."

Peter's words are very harsh. He does not think women are capable of living the greater Life—*macro bios*. He wants Mary Magdalene to stay in the kitchen and not join in studies with the men.

However, Jesus loves Mary and appreciates her views. According to some accounts, he kissed her. Peter, the leader of the disciples, couldn't stand Mary being near Jesus and taking care of him.

This is the situation confronting Jesus. There is dissension in the ranks and a possible threat to spreading the teachings and changing society. Coming upon a complaining Peter, Jesus says to him. "Don't worry. I will try to make her more yang. Then she will be like one of you."

By making Mary more yang (male), Jesus means making her stronger, healthier, and a person of higher judgment. Relative to each other, yin is weaker, slower, and darker. Yang is stronger, faster, and lighter. Everyone, male and female, has a balance of yin and yang energy. However, because men are more governed by incoming yang centripetal force from the sun, moon, stars, and distant galaxies, their consciousness is slightly more orderly, stable, and analytical. Because women are more governed by outward yin centrifugal force from the rotation of the earth on its axis, their consciousness is slightly more creative, spontaneous, and intuitive.

The way of thinking of men and women is very different. Because they are going in different directions (*see* Figure 23), the sexes often have a hard time understanding each other. This is especially true if they are eating improperly. Misperceptions

Figure 23. Heaven and Earth Forces in Man and Woman.

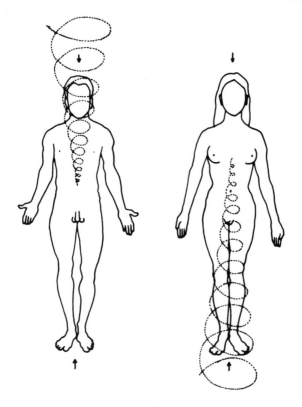

Though both sexes receive incoming *ki* or electromagnetic energy from heaven and earth, man, heaven's energy predominates, coming in counterclockwise through the spiral at the top of the head. In woman, earth energy is stronger, spiralling in through the uterus.

easily arise. Men think their way of thinking is better. They cannot understand why women don't reflect more and seem to be always acting on impulse. Women cannot understand why men take an eternity to think things through before acting or why they are so indecisive or fixed in their opinions.

Jesus understands that man and woman naturally complement and balance each other. He is trying to teach Peter that every one—male or female—who strengthens themselves and learns how to unify yin and yang will find eternal truth.

Later the Church was founded on Peter and Paul's interpretation of Jesus's teachings and Mary's was left out. Had the two main founders of Christianity really understood the laws and principles of dynamic change and harmony, centuries of misunderstanding between man and woman might have been avoided.

Now, after nearly two thousand years, we have the opportunity to restore that balance. Everyone, both male and female, should be able to cook wonderful, healthy meals and devote time to studying the marvelous Order of the Universe. As brothers and sisters of the infinite universe, let us together live as one in the Kingdom of Heaven.

Conclusion:
Making the Two One

Behind Jesus's teaching and view of life is the spiral—the dynamic unfolding of yin and yang, the two hands of God. The infinite universe endlessly transforms itself, polarizing, creating vibrations, manifesting itself into humans or other beings. These then reverse direction and return to the One. Millions and billions of differentiations are occurring every moment—attracting each other, antagonizing each other, complementing each other, supporting each other. This world is a world of differences. When we see this from our own small view, it appears to be a world of conflict and struggle, injustice and the absence of love. But that is a limited view. From a larger point of view, everything is complementary, everything is creating harmony. This smaller world we call the world of relativity. Life is short, ephemeral. It has a beginning and an end. But this relative world is really part of a bigger world. Things are constantly changing and moving toward that larger world or what we may call One, or God, or Infinity, or Eternal Harmony and Love.

The process is without beginning and end. It is like water streaming down creating ponds and lakes, then creating a river and finally an ocean before evaporating and creating clouds that bring rain again. In the cycle of growth, there are both yin and yang phases which operate at all times. In yang condensed form, water comes down forming ponds, lakes, and oceans, and then yin brings it back up again. The process may also be compared to a seed which produces a plant, which then creates seeds. Tight compact seeds give rise to tall, expanded plants and flowers. Then at the extremity of growth one force produces its opposite.

The ocean produces clouds. The flower produces seeds. When something expands to its limit, it produces yang or begins to contract. Similarly, when something contracts to its extreme point, it produces yin or begins to expand. So heaven and earth,

168

Table 2. Yin and Yang the in *Gospel of Thomas*.

	YANG	YIN
Location:	Heaven	Earth
	Above	Below
	Inside	Outside
	Near	Far
	First	Last
	Beginning	End
	Left	Right
Form:	Light	Darkness
	Morning	Evening
	Summer	Winter
	Empty	Full
	Body	Soul
	Flesh	Spirit
	Male	Female
Quality:	Living	Dead
	Small	Large
	Young	Old
	Hidden	Revealed
	Solitary	Divided
	Strong	[Weak]
	[Coarse]	Soft
Function:	Seeking	Finding
	Marveling	Troubling
	Giving	Receiving
	Moving	Resting
	Lending	Buying
	Loving	Hating
	Sowing	Reaping
Structure:	Lion	Human
	Serpent	Dove
	Fish	Bird
	Fox	Bird
	Crops	Weeds
	Tree	Fruit
	Roots	Vine
Relation:	Caesar	God
	Master	Servant
	Father	Mother
	Brother	Sister
	Thief	Owner

	Passerby	Guest
	Mote	Beam
Condition:	Seeing	Blind
	Poor	Rich
	Thirsty	Drunk
	Hungry	Satisfied
	Clean	Defiled
	New	Old
	Naked	Clothed

or yin and yang, create by combination, like the union of man and woman who combine to create new life.

This vast, wonderful, endless order Jesus calls the Kingdom of Heaven, the Kingdom of God, and the Kingdom of the Father. They all mean the same thing. In the sayings in the *Gospel of Thomas,* Jesus constantly refers to the complemental/antagonistic nature of life. For convenience, we have grouped together some of the qualities he mentions according to their relative yin and yang properties (*see* Table 2).

Jesus is always thinking in twos, in pairs, in terms of yin and yang. There are two horses, two bows, two masters, two wines, two garments, two resting on a bed, two in the field, two entering the bridal chamber. Over and over, he uses the phrase "making the two one."

By making the two one, Jesus means learning to see the unity of all things, to see life from all sides, from front and back, above and below, inside and outside.

Being able to make the two one is the entrance to the Kingdom of Heaven. It is not perfection, the "end" of our journey. It is simply growing up, reaching the stage of exercising intellectual judgment (*see* Figure 24). There are still many adventures to come in the social, philosophical, and supreme levels. But when we can make the two one, we begin to take responsibility for our health and happiness, our peace and freedom. We start to harmonize with the great spirallic current of life.

The key to reaching this level is proper eating. By eating good food, our yin/yang compass starts to work again. We leave behind hell—the injustice, sickness, ignorance, anger, and disorder

Figure 24. Living in the Kingdom of Heaven.

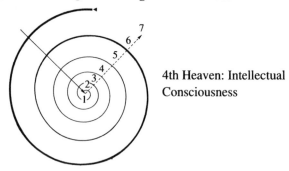

4th Heaven: Intellectual
Consciousness

You are consciously beginning to live in the Kingdom of Heaven when you understand and apply yang and yin, the universal laws of movement and rest, harmony and change.

of our own making. We do not taste death—that is, we do not become sad or bewildered and suffer during any stage of change in the endless process of transformation. Eventually as our understanding and practice deepen, we become one with the evermoving, everchanging Order of the Universe.

There are many ways to describe this change in consciousness. Jesus calls it entering the Kingdom of Heaven, being baptized in the Holy Spirit, becoming a Son of Man, returning to Paradise. We may simply call it growing up, graduating into adulthood, learning how to love.

Overcoming Dualism: Jesus continually tried to help people overcome their dualistic mentality and remember their common dream of one healthy, peaceful world. Like people today, people then divided everything into good and bad, right and wrong, just and unjust. They accepted the one, and rejected the other. It is this kind of thinking that was represented by eating from the Tree of Good and Evil. Dualistic thinking led to humanity's loss of health and freedom, symbolized by the expulsion from the Garden of Eden. In modern society, dualism leads to separation, alienation, and a lack of love on a personal level and to isolation, prejudice, and war on a social level.

Jesus embraced everyone and showed them how to cultivate the Tree of Life—unifying thinking. He taught people that they were already living in Paradise and were responsible for their own salvation. No one was excluded from his company. His disciples were drawn from all walks of life and segments of society. They included Pharisees and Scribes, Sadducees and Essenes, Zealot rebels and Roman soldiers. He especially welcomed those who were outcasts or rejected by society: publicans and sinners, tax collectors and prostitutes, the blind and dumb, the lepers and the possessed, Samaritans and strangers. Although he towered above everyone else in wisdom and judgment, Jesus did not act the part of a king but that of a servant. He constantly made the two one. He showed that to rule is to serve, to give is to receive. To turn the other cheek is to transform your enemy into a friend. To sacrifice your life for others is to become one with life as a whole.

During his lifetime, Jesus was widely misunderstood. Even most of his closest disciples continued to think that he was the Messiah or savior. His expression was a little too strong. He denied the absolute power of the Roman Empire because of the Unifying Principle which says that nothing is absolute or unchanging. He attracted people who were not in accord with conventional teachings, and the authorities decided to put him to death. But his spirit lived on. From a small seed, Christianity grew into a giant world religion. Jesus lost materially but triumphed spiritually. The Roman Empire became Christian. Yang changed into yin. Yin changed into yang.

People's memory of Jesus and his teachings also changed. Doubting Thomas alone appears to have grasped what Jesus was trying to express. His Gospel preserves the earliest, most original form of his sayings. His pen name, Didymus Judas Thomas ("Twin Judas Twin"), may refer to the primary twins in the universe—yin and yang. The repetition of "Twins" in his name wonderfully symbolizes "making the two one."

But after Thomas and the other disciples passed away, Jesus's teachings were altered. This process is evident in the New Testament. Many of Jesus's sayings and parables are found in the four

Gospels. But because their authors appear to have relied primarily on second- or third-hand sources, they did not understand the cosmological background to his teachings. They regarded Jesus as the Messiah or Christ and interpreted everything he said or did accordingly.

This is most evident in the parables and sayings that the *Gospel of Thomas* and the New Testament share in common. For example, let's look at the story of the wise fisherman. In the *Gospel of Thomas,* we read:

> And he said: "The Man [who is Living] is like a wise fisherman who cast his net into the sea. He drew it up from the deep full of small fishes. Among them he found a big, marvelous fish. That wise fisherman, he threw all the small fishes back into the sea. He chose the big fish without hesitation. Whoever has ears to hear, let him hear."—*Saying* 8

In the *Gospel of Matthew,* we read:

> Again, the Kingdom of heaven is like a net which was thrown into the sea and gathered fish of every kind; when it was full, men drew it ashore and sat down and sorted the good into vessels but threw away the bad. So it will be at the close of the age. The angels will come out and separate the evil from the righteous, and throw them into the furnace of fire; there men will weep and gnash their teeth.
>
> —13:47–50

In Thomas's account, the big fish represents God or One Infinity and its endless changing order, while the little fish represent phenomenal things. Jesus suggests that the wise fisherman seeks after the infinite life and lets the lesser fish go. He implies that it is foolish to trifle with transient things, but there is no sense of sin or immorality. In Matthew's account, the fish represent the evil and the righteous. There is a strong sense of morality. Apocalyptic imagery has been added. The parable has changed from a commentary on the process of eternal change to a sermon with terrifying images of hell and damnation.

In the same way, other teachings have been altered to reflect a dualistic rather than a unifying perspective. In the *Gospel of Thomas,* Jesus frequently mentions pairs and opposites to explain to his listeners how to unify things and make order. He uses common, everyday examples. He teaches his students that they can harmonize with the Order of the Universe by sorting fish, by broadcasting seed, by sifting grain, by bringing in animals from pasture, by selecting stones for building.

The point of each parable has to do with making balance, furthering order, appreciating the complementary/antagonistic nature of everything. There is no sense of good and evil, right and wrong, just and unjust. Jesus taught that the same harmonious process governs everything from the stars in the heavens to the smallest mustard grain on earth. But in the Bible and early Christian thought, the parables took on a messianic aura. Sorting yin and yang became sorting good and evil. The big fish became Christ the Savior, and the little fish became the baptized. The fruitful seed became the children of God and the weeds became the offspring of the Devil. The harvest became the close of the age, and the reapers became the angels. The wheat became a symbol of the just, the chaff a symbol of sinners. The sheep and goats came to stand for the saved and the damned.

The original, clear sayings of Jesus took on dualistic overtones as they passed through the hands of different authors, editors, and early Church authorities. The Spiral of Life was forgotten. Its graceful curves became a straight line. The Spiral of Physicalization was replaced by the Fall of Man. The Spiral of Spiritualization was replaced by the resurrection of the dead at the Last Judgment. The natural connection between the descending and ascending curves of life was broken. Spirit and matter became eternal opposites. In the *Gospel of Thomas,* Jesus is very simple, intuitive, practical, universal. In the other Gospels, he is more abstract, conceptual, emotional, particular.

This narrowing of vision is party due to the influence of Iranian dualism, Middle Eastern mystery religions, Gnosticism, and other philosophies of the day. But also it is clear that the way of eating of those who contributed to the New Testament was much richer and more complex than that of Jesus, Thomas, and the original disciples. Jesus's manner and expression were very direct. Those of the four Gospels, Paul, Peter, and the early Church were more complicated. Jesus taught his students to unify past, present, and future. The Apostle Paul made a sharp contrast between the present era and the New Age to come. Jesus taught that the Kingdom of Heaven is always present. The New Testament writers portray it as a future event. Jesus taught that Paradise—the union of yin and yang in harmony, in love— is open to everyone. The theologians preached that it was available only to the select few.

After his death, a big church grew up in Jesus's name. But over the centuries, the original teachings were lost, the way of eating was forgotten, and the followers of the new religion could no longer heal people. Science and medicine became the new Messiah, promising to restore lost Paradise.

Although the religion named after him turned into its opposite, Jesus's spirit of love remained. Even traces of the spiral survived in symbols such as the Star of David, the cross, the menorah, and the crozier or bishop's staff (*see* Figure 25).

Now almost two thousand years later, the *Gospel of Thomas* preserving Jesus's authentic voice has been recovered. Whoever has ears—twin spirals—to hear, let them hear.

Figure 25. Symbols of the Spiral.

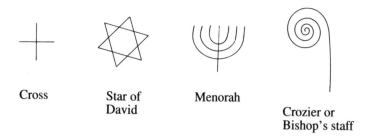

Cross

Star of
David

Menorah

Crozier or
Bishop's staff

Appendix:

Principles and Laws of the Order of the Universe

The universal principles and laws of change have been understood by traditional cultures and civilizations in East and West, North and South. Since ancient times, they have been enshrined in various ways in their scriptures, calendars and myths, systems of agriculture and food production, cuisine and dietary pattern, art and architecture, and the healing arts. In the modern age, the principles and laws of balance and harmony have been rediscovered and expressed by various philosophers, scientists, authors, and artists. In this century, they were comprehensively outlined by George Ohsawa and further simplified by the author and his associates through their experiences and observations of nature and society during the past thirty-five years.

The seven principles and twelve laws are listed below followed by selected quotations from the *Gospel of Thomas* and the Bible.

The Seven Principles

1. *Everything is a differentiation of One Infinity.*

"Hear, O Israel: The Lord, our God, is one . . ."
—*Deuteronomy* 6: 4

Jesus said: "I am the light that is above them all. I am the Whole. The Whole came forth from Me, and the Whole returns to Me. Cleave a piece of wood, I am there. Raise the stone, and you shall find Me there."—*Gospel of Thomas,* 77

2. *Everything changes.*

"To everything there is a season, and a time to every purpose under the heaven." —*Ecclesiastes* 3:1

"Jesus said: This heaven will pass away and the one above it will pass away . . . " —*Gospel of Thomas,* 11

3. *All antagonisms are complementary.*

"Do you not understand that he who made the inside is also he who made the outside?" —*Gospel of Thomas,* 89

"And we know that all things work together for good to them that love God . . . " —*Romans* 8:28.

4. *There is nothing identical.*

"Many, O Lord my God, are thy wonderful works which thou hast done . . . they are more than can be numbered."

—*Psalms* 40: 5

"There is one glory of the sun, and another glory of the moon, and another glory of the stars; for one star differeth from another star in glory." —*I Corinthians* 15:41

5. *What has a front has a back.*

"Blessed are the poor, for yours is the Kingdom of Heaven."
—*Gospel of Thomas,* 54

"Jesus said: Blessed is the man who has suffered, he has found Life." —*Gospel of Thomas,* 58

"Jesus said: Blessed are those who have been persecuted in their hearts; for they have truly known the Father."
—*Gospel of Thomas,* 69

6. *The bigger the front, the bigger the back.*

Jesus said: "Why did you come into the wilderness? To see a reed blowing in the wind? And to see a man clothed in soft garments? [Behold,] your kings and your powerful ones are those who are clothed in soft [garments] and yet they will not be able to know the truth." —*Gospel of Thomas,* 78

"He hath put down the mighty from their seats, and exalted them of low degree. He filled the hungry with good things; and the rich he hath sent empty away." —*Luke* 1:52–53

7. *What has a beginning has an end.*

"For where the beginning is, there the end will be."
—*Gospel of Thomas,* 18

"Heaven and earth shall pass away: but My words shall not pass away." —*Mark* 13:31

The Twelve Laws

1. *One Infinity manifests itself into complementary and antagonistic tendencies, yin and yang, in its endless change.*

"In the beginning, God created the heaven and the earth."
—*Genesis,* 1:1

"If they ask you: 'What is the sign of your Father in you?,' say to them: 'It is movement and rest.' "
—*Gospel of Thomas,* 50

178

2. *Yin and yang are manifested continuously from the eternal movement of one infinite universe.*

"I form the light, and create darkness; I make peace, and create evil: I the Lord do all these things." —*Isaiah* 45:7

3. *Yin represents centrifugality. Yang represents centripetality. Yin and yang together produce energy and all phenomena.*

"Look upon all the works of the most high. They, likewise, are in pairs, one the opposite of the other."
—*Ecclesiasticus* 33:15

4. *Yin attracts yang. Yang attracts yin.*

"The wolf also shall dwell with the lamb, and the leopard shall lie down with the kid; and the calf and the young lion and the fatling together . . . " —*Isaiah* 11:6

5. *Yin repels yin. Yang repels yang.*

"Jesus said: No prophet is honored in his village, no physician heals those who know him." —*Gospel of Thomas*, 31

6. *Yin and yang combined in varying proportions produce different phenomena. The attraction and repulsion among phenomena is proportional to the difference of the yin and yang forces.*

Jesus said: "No man drinks old wine and immediately desires to drink new wine. New wine is not put into old wineskins lest they burst, nor old wine into a new wineskin, lest it spoil it. An old patch is not sewn on a new garment, because it would tear."
—*Gospel of Thomas*, 47

"My grace is sufficient for thee: for my strength is made perfect in weakness." —*II Corinthians* 12:9

7. *All phenomena are ephemeral, constantly changing their constitution of yin and yang forces; yin changes into yang, yang changes into yin.*

"Every valley shall be exalted, and every mountain and hill shall be made low: and the crooked shall be made straight, and the rough places plain." —*Isaiah* 40:4

Jesus said: "The Kingdom of the [Father] is like a woman who was carrying a jar full of flour. While she was walking on a road far from home, the handle of the jar broke. The flour spilled out behind her on the road. She did not know it, as she was not aware anything was wrong. When she arrived home, she put down the jar and found it empty." —*Gospel of Thomas,* 97

8. *Nothing is solely yin or solely yang. Everything is composed of both tendencies in varying degrees.*

"For the elements were changed in themselves by a kind of harmony . . . The fire had power in the water, forgetting his own virtue: and the water forgot his own quenching nature."
    —*Wisdom of Solomon* 19:18–20

Simon Peter said to them: "Let Mary leave us, because women are not worthy of Life." Jesus said: "Behold, I shall guide her and make her male, that she too may become a living spirit like you men. For every woman who makes herself male shall enter the Kingdom of Heaven." —*Gospel of Thomas*, 114

9. *There is nothing neutral. Either yin or yang is in excess in every occurrence.*

Jesus said: "It is impossible for a man to mount two horses and to draw two bows. And it is impossible for a servant to serve two masters, lest he honor the one and show disrespect to the other." —*Gospel of Thomas*, 47

10. *Large yin attracts small yin. Large yang attracts small yang.*

Jesus said: "You see the mote that is in your brother's eye, but you do not see the beam that is in your own eye."
—*Gospel of Thomas*, 26

11. *Extreme yin produces yang, and extreme yang produces yin.*

Jesus said: "Blessed is the lion that the man devours and the lion will become human. Cursed is the man whom the lion devours and [the man will become lion]." —*Gospel of Thomas*, 7

"Whosoever shall exalt himself shall be abased; and he that shall humble himself shall be exalted." —*Matthew* 23:12

12. *All physical manifestations are yang at the center, and yin at the periphery.*

The disciples said to Jesus: "Tell us what the Kingdom of Heaven is like." He said to them: "It is like a mustard-seed, the smallest of all seeds. But when it falls on the tilled soil, it puts forth a large branch and becomes shelter for the birds of the air."
—*Gospel of Thomas*, 20

Jesus said: "He who is near to Me is near to the fire, and he who is far from Me is far from the Kingdom."
—*Gospel of Thomas*, 82

Bibliography

Crossan, John Dominic, ed. *Sayings Parallels*. Philadelphia: Fortress Press, 1986.

Funk, Robert W., ed. *New Gospel Parallels*. Vol. 1. Philadelphia: Fortress Press, 1985.

The Gnostic Scriptures: A New Translation. Translated by Bently Layton. New York: Doubleday, 1987.

Guillaumont, A., H.C. Peuch, G. Quispel, W. Till, and Yasah 'Abd Al Masih. *The Gospel According to Thomas*. San Francisco: Harper and Row, 1959.

Holy Bible. King James Version, 1611.

Holy Bible. Revised Standard Version. National Council of Churches, 1946, 1952.

Ineson, Rev. John. *The Way of Life: Macrobiotics and the Spirit of Christianity*. Tokyo and New York: Japan Publications, Inc., 1986.

The Interpreter's Dictionary of the Bible. Nashville: Abingdon, 1962, 1976.

Iyer, Pico. *The Gospel According to Thomas*. New York: Concord Grove Press, 1983.

Jack, Alex. "Jesus's Legendary Travels in the Orient." *East West Journal* (January 1978): 76–87.

—— "Jesus and the Essene Christ." *East West Journal* (February, 1978): 76–85.

—— "Jesus and Women." *East West Journal* (May, 1978): 62–71.

—— *Let Food Be Thy Medicine*. Becket, Mass.: One Peaceful World Press, 1991.

—— *The New Age Dictionary*. Tokyo and New York: Japan Publications, Inc., 1990.

—— "The Secret of the Loaves and Fishes." *East West Journal* (April 1978): 36–43.

Jack, Gale, with Alex Jack. *Promenade Home: Macrobiotics and Women's Health*. Tokyo and New York: Japan Publications, Inc., 1988.

The Jerusalem Bible. New York: Darton, Longman & Todd and Doubleday, 1966.

Koester, Helmet. *Ancient Christian Gospels*. London: SCM Press, 1990.

Kushi, Aveline, with Alex Jack. *Aveline Kushi's Complete Guide to Macrobiotic Cooking for Health, Harmony, and Peace*. New York: Warner Books, 1985.

—— *Aveline: The Life and Dream of the Woman Behind Macrobiotics Today*. Tokyo and New York: Japan Publications, Inc., 1988.

Kushi, Michio, with Alex Jack. *The Book of Macrobiotics: The Universal Way of Health, Happiness and Peace*. Tokyo and New York: Japan Publications, Inc., 1987 (Rev. ed.).

—— *The Cancer-Prevention Diet*. New York: St. Martin's Press, 1983.

—— *Diet for a Strong Heart*. New York: St. Martin's Press, 1985.

—— *One Peaceful World*. New York: St. Martin's Press, 1987.

Kushi, Michio and Aveline, with Alex Jack. *Food Governs Your Destiny: The Teachings of Namboku Mizuno*. Tokyo and New York: Japan Publications, Inc., 1991.

—— *Macrobiotic Diet*. Tokyo and New York: Japan Publications, Inc., 1985.

Meyer, Marvin. *The Secret Teachings of Jesus*. New York: Vintage Books, 1986.

The New English Bible. London: Oxford University Press and Cambridge University Press, 1961, 1970.

The New Jewish Version. The Jewish Publications Society, 1967 (Rev. ed.).

Ohsawa, George. *The Art of Peace*. Oroville, Calif.: George Ohsawa Macrobiotic Foundation, 1990.

Robinson, James, ed. *The Nag Hammadi Library in English*. New York: Harper and Row, 1977, 1988.

Ross, Hugh McGregor. *The Gospel of Thomas*. York, England: William Sessions Ltd., 1987.

Schweitzer, Albert. *The Mystery of the Kingdom of Heaven*, 1914; English translation, Schocken Books, 1970.

The Septuagint Version. London: S. Bagster & Sons, 1900.

Smith, Richard. *A Concise Coptic-English Lexicon.* Grand Rapids, Michigan: William B. Eerdmans, 1983.

Winterhalter, Robert. *The Fifth Gospel.* New York: Harper and Row, 1988.

Macrobiotic Resources

For information on macrobiotic publishing activities in the United States and abroad, please contact:

One Peaceful World
Box 10
Becket, Mass. 01223
(413) 623-2322

For information on Michio Kushi's Spiritual Development Seminars at which the *Gospel of Thomas*, the Bible, and other spiritual classics are discussed, please contact:

Kushi Institute
Box 7
Becket, Mass. 01223
(413) 623-5741

About the Authors

Michio Kushi was born into a family of educators in Japan on May 17, 1926. As a child, he lived for a time in Hiroshima, where his father was a professor of history at the university, specializing in the Renaissance. His mother taught high school and later served as a judge in the family court in Tokyo.

After completing his studies in international law at Tokyo University, Michio Kushi came to the United States in 1949 to pursue world government studies and study and teach macrobiotics. In the early 1960s, he and his wife, Aveline, founded Erewhon, the nation's pioneer natural foods company. During the last twenty-five years, he has lectured around the world on health, diet, and consciousness and the peaceful meeting of East and West. In 1971 his students founded the *East West Journal,* and in the following year the East West Foundation was started to spread macrobiotic education and research. In 1978, he and his wife started the Kushi Institute, an educational organization for the training of macrobiotic teachers and cooks, with affiliates in various countries.

In recent years, Michio Kushi has met with government and social leaders at the United Nations, the World Health Organization, UNESCO, the White House, and in many world capitals. His seminars and lectures on a dietary approach to degenerative disease and the reconstruction of modern humanity have attracted thousands of doctors, nurses, nutritionists, and other health care professionals. Medical researchers at Harvard Medical School, the Framingham Heart Study, Boston University, Columbia-Presbyterian Hospital in New York, and elsewhere have researched the benefits of the macrobiotic diet. The Lemuel Shattuck Hospital in Boston, the Powhatan State Penitentiary near Richmond, Virginia, and other institutions began serving macrobiotic food prepared by his students. On a visit to Africa in 1987, he was invited by the government of the Congo to set up a macrobiotic dietary program to prevent AIDS, and subsequently he has advised several other governments on public health, food, and agriculture. With his wife, Aveline, he resides in Brookline and Becket, Massachusetts.

Alex Jack was born in Chicago in 1945, the year of the discovery of the *Gospel of Thomas.* The son, grandson, and great-grandson of Unitarian and Congregational ministers, he was also influenced by Jewish and Catholic ancestry. As a child he accompanied his father to a world peace conference in Japan and in high school attended Friends Meeting. After graduating from Oberlin College with a degree in philosophy, he attended seminary and majored in Biblical studies. In the 1960s, he served as a civil rights worker in the South, helped atomic-bomb survivors in Hiroshima organize an arts festival, and reported on the war in Vietnam. In the 1970s, he became associated with the Kushis and served as editor-in-chief of the *East West Journal* and director of the Kushi Institute of the Berkshires. His career as an author, journalist, and teacher has taken him to India, China, the Soviet Union, and many other countries. He is currently the director of One Peaceful World, an international macrobiotic information network and friendship society, in Becket, Massachusetts, where he lives with his wife. Alex is the author or co-author of several books including *The Cancer-Prevention Diet, Aveline Kushi's Complete Guide to Macrobiotic Cooking,* and *Let Food Be Thy Medicine.*

Index

190

192

194

Scriptural Index

Hebrew Bible

New Testament

Intertestamental Literature

Tao Te Ching